CHAMPIONSHIP BEHAVIORS

A MODEL FOR COMPETITIVE
EXCELLENCE IN SPORTS

HUGH McCUTCHEON

FOREWORD BY THAD LEVINE

TRIUMPH
BOOKS

Library of Congress Cataloging-in-Publication Data available upon request.

This book is available in quantity at special discounts for your group or organization. For further information, contact:

Triumph Books LLC
814 North Franklin Street
Chicago, Illinois 60610
(312) 337-0747
www.triumphbooks.com

Printed in U.S.A.
ISBN: 978-1-62937-957-9
Design and editorial production by Alex Lubertozzi

Contents

Foreword

One of the first times I met Hugh, we sat shoulder to shoulder engrossed in a deep conversation while assessing the spectacle that played out in front of us. We were watching our respective sons play their hearts out in a highly contested nine-and-under basketball game. Cognizant of Hugh's exceptional coaching reputation, I had steeled myself for a technical conversation of how to properly implement the one-three-one zone defense. Instead, Hugh led me in a master class in how sports provide an invaluable forum especially for children to hone their emotional control skills, and how much those skills serve as an invaluable foundation for not only athletic, but also academic, professional, and familial achievements.

The referee blew a shrill whistle and registered a foul. In response to the perceived injustice, the aggrieved player slammed down the ball as unwanted tears uncontrollably streaked down his face. As members of the semi-packed field-house aspired to distance themselves from a child wallowing in the throes of immaturity, Hugh energetically spoke of the amazing opportunity that this moment of emotional adversity presented for shaping this boy not only as an athlete but more importantly as a young man. Hugh saw past the frenzied outburst and identified an opportunity for authentic growth.

I have been blessed to hear Hugh share his wisdom professionally as a valued consultant to the Minnesota Twins, academically as a TED speaker, and socially as a dear friend. Hugh has helped shape me as a coach, father, husband, colleague, and leader in a highly competitive professional sports industry. Hugh's teachings transcend sport and apply brilliantly to parenting and business. As such, *Championship Behaviors*, while grounded in athletics, equips readers with tools to not only survive but also thrive across all facets of life.

Hugh's career has been inextricably connected to competitive excellence at the professional, collegiate, and Olympic levels, but he would be the first to urge people not to singularly associate success on the court with success as a coach. Quite to the contrary, in *Championship Behaviors*, Hugh offers an enlightened view of sports as a vehicle to develop skills to optimize athletes' contributions to the betterment of society. Hugh's commitment to develop not only athletes but, more importantly, dynamic people is his superpower.

Drawing on decades of coaching experience and achievements, Hugh has refined what he describes as the three pillars of development: physical, mental, and social. Most coaches focus primarily, if not exclusively, on physical talent, because they are preoccupied with wins and losses—the alleged ultimate outcome of competition. Hugh believes that if you value the process, coaches must invest in developing mental and social skills in addition to physical skills. Scientific research proves that physical skill is not simply innate, but that it can be developed through effective and efficient practice methods. Mental skills span focus and decision-making to emotional control. Social skills speak to a player's dedication to the team above self and commitment to invest in the development of one's teammates and share in their challenges. A championship-caliber player marries refined physical skills with superior mental resiliency and the unflagging social awareness to elevate their own performance and the performance of teammates. A championship coach provides players with superior resources and a safe environment rich with competitive opportunities to improve these championship behaviors.

Hugh sets an elite standard of excellence for coaches. He establishes the cornerstones of championship-caliber coaching as heightened awareness and the ability to teach, coach, and mentor. Those embracing the skill of coaching alone may fall short of providing the resources necessary for an athlete to grow, develop, and achieve excellence. By training in game-like environments, effective learning can enhance an athlete's ability to refine talent as well as harness emotional control. Exceptional coaches maximize their athletes' and teams' ability to achieve at the highest level. Extraordinary mentors foster safe, trustworthy environments and have unparalleled abilities to connect with the heads and the hearts of their athletes.

Hugh has expertly used sports to craft a proven paradigm of physical, mental, and social development. Whether readers are athletes seeking to benefit from Hugh's decades of coaching wisdom; coaches; business leaders aspiring to improve their teaching, coaching, and mentoring skills; or parents eager to provide their children with the tools to be the best version of themselves, *Championship Behaviors* provides the perfect blueprint.

—Thad Levine
Senior VP and General Manager
Minnesota Twins

Preface

My Pursuit of Excellence

In 1985, I started playing competitive volleyball, and at the ripe old age of 15, I was a relative latecomer to it.

I started playing volleyball because of my basketball coach. We were warming up for a game, and I decided that I'd try to dunk the basketball. It certainly wasn't going to involve any slamming, but maybe if everything lined up, I could get the ball to sneak over the edge of the rim with two hands. (I couldn't palm the basketball at the time.) Sure enough, to everyone's surprise—including mine—I did just that. Emboldened, I decided to have another go the next time around, but this time I was really going to put the boosters on. I was able to dunk again, just barely, but the extra boost had me flying off-balance past the rim, and I grabbed on tight so I wouldn't swing all the way through and land on my back. I landed safely on my feet and went back to the end of the line.

My coach was not happy. "Showboating" was apparently what I was doing—swinging on the rim—and there was no room for that! The dunk itself seemed to be of little to no consequence, and the penalty for my efforts was the threat of having to buy a new basketball rim, because apparently my 140-pound frame may have bent it! Money was tight in the McCutcheon household, and $100 for a new rim was not really an option. So I apologized and tried to convince him of my innocent intentions, but was met with only doubting looks and the threat of a bill showing up at home. It was a bummer. I liked basketball, but if this is how the coach was going to be, I figured I'd go and try something else. The guys on the volleyball team seemed cool, and the coach was my physics teacher, and he seemed all right. So I tried out, made the team, and that's how all of this began.

New Zealand is by no means a volleyball powerhouse. It's the home of the All Blacks, and rugby is our sport. There's also America's Cup yachting, Commonwealth sports like cricket and netball, basketball (Steven Adams!), soccer, bungee jumping, zorbing, hobbits . . . and then further down the list is volleyball.

In 1988, I was sitting on my couch in Christchurch, watching channel 1 (of two TV channels that were offered at that time), which was broadcasting the men's volleyball final from the Summer Olympic Games in Seoul. I watched the USA men defeat Russia in four sets to win the gold medal, and I remember thinking how awesome the whole thing was: the Olympics, Olympic volleyball, and winning a gold medal. Little did I know that 20 years later I'd get to coach the USA men to that same result—an unlikely turn of events considering my humble volleyball beginnings.

I came to America in 1990 to play volleyball. Brigham Young University recruited me, and while playing and coaching there, I earned three different degrees: a BS in physical education with an emphasis in coaching, an MS in exercise science with a minor in statistics, and an MBA.

I played for three years at BYU. (I had already attended the University of Canterbury in Christchurch, New Zealand, for two years, and the NCAA gives athletes five years to complete four seasons of competition, once they've enrolled as full-time students.) It was a challenging transition made more challenging by the fact that our team wasn't very good. We went 2–27 that first season. It got better, and after graduating with my bachelor's degree, I played professionally for a couple of years in Finland and then in Japan. As much as I enjoyed playing, I knew it wasn't going to provide me any long-term security, so I stopped after my season with the Zojirushi Tuff-Boyz in Osaka and returned to BYU to start my first graduate degree, with the intent of later pursuing a PhD. I also began coaching as an assistant coach with the BYU men, initially as a means to this academic end, but I quickly realized that coaching was going to be a better path for me than academia, hence the MBA. Coaching can be a fickle business, so I figured a "real world" qualification would be a better Plan B than exercise science and statistics. While coaching at BYU, we won two NCAA national championships in 1999 and 2001. We'd come a long way from 2–27.

During the summers of 1999 and 2000, I was asked to be the head coach of the USA Youth and Junior National Teams, and in 2001 I received an invitation to help coach the USA men's team in Colorado Springs, which I accepted. For the next two years, I coached a professional team in Europe (the Vienna HotVolleys) during the winters and then assisted with the USA men during the summers. In 2003, I became a full-time assistant coach with the USA men's team, and we went on to finish fourth at the 2004 Athens Olympic Games. A strong, but heart-aching finish.

After Athens I was encouraged to apply for the USA men's head coaching job, which I did—but not without a fair amount of thought and introspection. I was fortunate enough to get the position, and we ended up winning the 2008 Olympic Games in Beijing. Having achieved everything we had set out to do with the USA men, I asked if USA Volleyball would consider allowing me to coach the USA women for the 2012 quadrennial. I wanted to change because the idea of coaching the USA women in a similar style to that of the USA men (who had won three Olympic gold medals in volleyball while the women had, at that point, not yet reached the top of the podium) seemed like an intriguing challenge. They supported the change, and we had a great run. We were ranked No. 1 in the world going into the Olympics and ended up winning a silver medal in London.

I decided to leave USA Volleyball after the 2012 Games and started coaching women's volleyball at the University of Minnesota. This time the reason for change was personal. My wife and I had started our family, and by the time the London Olympics had ended, we had two children, aged two-and-a-half years and six months. The goal had always been to try to be No. 1 Dad, not No. 1 Coach, and the rigor of international volleyball was real. The travel demands were heavy, and so coaching collegiately seemed like it could afford us more balance and more family time. After all, a three-day trip to Indiana was easier to manage than a 30-day tour in Asia.

During my time at Minnesota, we've had solid competitive success. We've been to three Final Fours and won the Big Ten Conference a couple of times. I was also inducted into the International Volleyball Hall of Fame in 2018. It's been an eventful and successful journey.

As a player, volleyball had my heart. Having come to the game later in life than most, I felt a real urgency to improve and had a passion to succeed. I had to out-work and out-learn my peers, but I didn't really know how. Fortunately, I was able to come to the United States and play for Dr. Carl McGown, a volleyball coach and former professor of motor learning, who helped teach me the game and helped me learn more about what effective and efficient training methods looked like.

As a coach, volleyball had my head. The whole thing was a seemingly endless puzzle with ever-changing pieces. I coached with Carl while attending graduate school, and then, while coaching the national teams, I enlisted the help of Dr. Ken Ravizza, a pioneer in the world of sports psychology whose insights into the mental game were revolutionary. I also had the privilege of connecting with Dr. Anders Ericsson, the world's foremost researcher on deliberate practice and expertise.

My time with these greats in their respective fields combined with my own unique experiences, and the influence of countless others I have been fortunate enough to work with over my career, helped me to formulate a more comprehensive approach to competitive excellence. This process was galvanized by the consistent level of competitive success we were able to achieve over the 26 years of coaching teams of men and women at the college, professional, and international level.

If applying these principles and methods to different populations worked in my pursuit of competitive excellence, I'm sure they can work for you as well. Whether you're an athlete, a coach, or someone who's hoping to better understand the process of competitive excellence, I am sure you will learn things in these pages that will help you to achieve your goals.

Introduction

What Are Championship Behaviors?

The goal of this book is to help people. Specifically, to help people who want to achieve significant outcomes in sports, where *significant* means to strive for an outcome that will require work and change. Something beyond their current abilities.

It is a practical guide to goal achievement, through a process of competitive excellence that speaks to the art and the science of that pursuit. We talk about principles and methods that have led to efficient and effective learning and consistent competitive success. We cite some research but, more importantly, discuss how this research applies and explain why you should apply it. We also discuss the humanity of sports, the personal challenges and the interpersonal connections that sports afford us, as well as the significant benefits that come from both. The stuff that makes sports great.

The path to achievement in sports, particularly regarding coaching and skill development, needs clearer definition—and that is a main impetus for writing this book. To start, merely from an academic perspective, there isn't a strong educational pathway in coaching. Currently 57 out of roughly 5,300 colleges and universities in the United States offer it as an undergraduate program,[1] and as a result it is easy to see why coaching tends to be tradition-based. People tend to coach the way they were coached, as opposed to using methods based in current best practice and scientific rigor. Tradition is important—we certainly should respect it—but it should never be the reason for doing anything, unless it's the right reason.

We have rigorous academic requirements for our teachers, who need university degrees and professional certifications before they can even step into a classroom. But our coaches may not have studied anything to do with biomechanics or exercise science. They may not have studied anything to do with coaching or teaching. Their only qualification, in fact, may be that they played the sport, perhaps at a good level, and somehow that's sufficient.

If you are a coach, this book might stimulate some thought, and that's all I'm really trying to do here, get people to think a little. I'm not going to tell you right from wrong, but I will talk to you about efficient and effective methods that you should consider. If you are an athlete, this book will give the process of skill acquisition and skill application some structure. You'll have a better understanding of how to approach practice, learning, and the moment of competition. If you are a parent of an athlete and are investing your time and money in your child's sport, this book will help you to evaluate the services that you're paying for. It might also offer some perspective on the significant value sports can add to your young athlete's life.

I called this book *Championship Behaviors* because championship results take championship behaviors. It's as simple as that. If you want to achieve excellence in sports, you have to learn to act "as if." I might like to go to the moon, but if I'm not prepared to do the immense amount of work it takes to become an astronaut, a moon landing seems, at the very least, unlikely. If you want to achieve something significant in sports, this book will give the process of competitive excellence and achievement a clearly defined framework that is applicable and scalable to any age or any level.

To start, let's discuss in broad terms the value of sports in our society. It doesn't seem as though many people "play" sports anymore. It's increasingly gone from a recreation or pastime to a business, a business that is based almost exclusively on outcomes. If we just focus on competitive sports, not the health and wellness industry or the sports betting industry, our major professional sports are incredibly effective at generating revenue. The trickle-down influence on the lower levels of sports, based on the dream of achieving sporting fame and financial security, is very real. A select few professional athletes sign multi-year contracts for hundreds of millions of dollars. Even fewer Olympic champions leverage their athletic success into financially lucrative endorsement deals. This level of sporting success should be celebrated. These athletes have dedicated years of their lives to becoming the embodiment of athletic achievement and success, and they also become the standard to which everyone aspires. They are the sporting dream realized.

But how do you live that dream? How do people achieve such extraordinary levels of skill and competitive success? Are they born like that? Do people help them? And, if so, who are these people? The answer to all of this is complicated, but what is clear is that both the athlete and the coach have a part to play in this pursuit of competitive excellence, and the dream, no matter how unlikely it is to come to fruition, can often become the focus of years and years of training and competition. Training and competition that come at a price that includes, at the very least, real costs and opportunity costs.

The narrative around this pursuit of sporting achievement starts all too early. You have to get the right start in youth sports, the earlier the better. If you start too late, you'll never make it. Without years of youth sports training and experience you'll struggle to make the high school team or the best Amateur Athletic Union (AAU)/club teams. In turn, being selected to those teams will give you the best chance to be recruited to a college program. There might also be discussions around private lessons, strength and conditioning, or speed and quickness training. If you can get into the right college (where "right" might be in reference to the division, or conference, or school, or program, or coach), that will increase your chances of playing professionally or competing in the Olympics.

All these levels of instruction and competition cost time and money, and subsequently sports are a massive economic engine that benefits many different entities. But what about the athletes? How do we know if they are on the right path to the promised land of athletic achievement? How do the coaches of these athletes ensure they are applying the most effective and efficient methods to guide their athletes to achieve significant outcomes? This book will help to answer those questions.

There currently isn't a comprehensive, codified structure for the process of achieving competitive excellence in sports— or any way to objectively assess or evaluate whether the quality of the coaching, instruction, or competition that you're paying for is worth the money. Apart from the dream, what exactly is everyone selling? I think that people believe, or are led to believe, that their investments at all these different levels will help their athlete make it to the next level, the next rung on the ladder toward athletic fame and fortune. That the youth sports program is the best preparation for your high school and AAU/ club career, and that your high school and AAU/club team is the best place to be developed and seen so that the scholarship offer will come. And that the scholarship will provide, not just a free education, but the best environment to prepare for the professional or Olympic arena.

Let's have a look at the numbers—not just the odds of making it pro but what the return on investment actually looks like. The first potential financial benefit from an investment in youth and high school AAU/club sports is an NCAA college scholarship. The popular notion is that all NCAA athletic scholarships are full grant-in-aide, or full-ride, scholarships that cover the student-athletes' tuition and fees, textbooks, room and board, and include a cost-of-attendance allowance. There are some sports that can only award full rides, but there are many that can award either full or partial scholarships.

The percentage of high school or AAU/club participants across all sports who receive some type of athletically related financial aid (scholarship assistance) to participate in intercollegiate athletics has been estimated to be around 2 percent, according to the NCAA website. This number not only includes full grant-in-aid scholarships, it's any form of athletically related financial aid that's awarded. So the student-athlete might only be getting their textbooks paid for by the university and they, or their family, are financially responsible for the rest. The average amount of athletically related financial aid given to NCAA Division 1 and Division 2 student-athletes (NCAA Division 3 schools do not offer athletic scholarships) has been estimated to be around $13,000 per year.[2]

We would be remiss not to mention the potential compensation college athletes can now receive through their name, image, and likeness (NIL) and as a consequence of the *NCAA v. Alston* lawsuit. The NCAA rule changes and Supreme Court decision are relatively new in the college sports world and are still not clearly defined in terms of how they're applied or enforced. Needless to say, there are now more student-athletes making money from college sports than there were when the latest NCAA scholarship data, which we're using as a basis for this discussion, was collected in 2020.

What about making it to the pros? If we use NCAA college football as our first example, what are the chances of getting drafted? This recent 2020 NCAA study stated that there were close to 74,000 athletes competing in college football. Of those 74,000, approximately 16,400 were draft eligible, but only 254 athletes were drafted by the NFL. That's 1.55 percent of draft-eligible athletes, and only 0.34 percent of all NCAA football participants, who make it.

In NCAA basketball, the odds were even smaller. There were close to 19,000 athletes on the men's side, of whom approximately 4,200 were draft eligible. On average, 52 NCAA athletes are drafted by the NBA each year. (There are 60 picks, and the other eight tend to go to athletes outside of the collegiate system.) That's 1.24 percent of all draft eligible athletes, and only 0.27 percent of all NCAA men's basketball participants, getting drafted.

In NCAA women's basketball, there were approximately 16,500 athletes participating, of which 3,700 were deemed to be draft eligible. Of the 36 total draft picks in the WNBA, 31 went to NCAA collegiate athletes and, like the men, the other five picks went to athletes outside of the collegiate system. That's 0.84 percent of draft-eligible athletes and 0.19 percent of all women's college basketball athletes making it to the league each year.

These are the odds of going from college to the pros; the odds of making it from high school to the pros get even smaller. Again, if we use the NCAA data from 2020 and use football as the example, there were 1,000,613 high school football players in the United States and 7.3 percent of those high school players (or 73,712) were recruited to play in all three divisions of NCAA football (2.9 percent, or 29,018, competed at the Division 1 level). Remember, only 1.55 percent of draft-eligible players and 0.34 percent of all NCAA football players will get drafted.

Only 0.025 percent of the original population of 1,000,613 high school football players will get drafted by the NFL. That's approximately one athlete out of every 3,939 who play.

Even then, being a "successful" professional athlete is yet another hurdle to overcome. Getting drafted is just getting drafted; the data does not take into consideration other factors such as how long the athlete is in the league, or whether they got paid millions of dollars or league minimum.

If that's the reality, what about the dream? Another NCAA study from 2019 found that 41 percent of college football athletes surveyed believed that it was "somewhat likely" or "likely" they would get drafted to the NFL. In addition, that same study found that this narrative of athletic success had been present in these athletes' lives since their time in youth sports. In fact, 61 percent of these NCAA football athletes said that when they were young, they had been told by their families that they were expected to play collegiately, and 31 percent of the athletes' families had also expressed the expectation that the child would play football professionally. That's a lot for a kid to carry around.

We should pause for moment here and acknowledge the fairly large discrepancy between the perception of the odds of making it to the NFL and the reality: 41 percent of college football athletes think it's at least "somewhat likely" they'll get drafted, but only 0.34 percent actually make it, or about 1 in 300. And approximately one-third of families express the expectation to their youth-sports athlete that they will play professional football when the odds of making it from high school—not youth sports—are closer to 1 in 4,000. That's a pretty big difference.

The next consideration in all of this, which is beyond the scope of this book but bears mentioning, is the collateral damage to a person whose childhood was consumed with sports but did not produce the professional outcomes they were promised or expected. They didn't go pro, even with families that supported them from an early age and told them that a professional career was a possible, maybe even probable, outcome. As we can see, the percentage of athletes who do make it is extremely small. But the athletes aren't told that; they don't know that the deck was stacked against them all along. They feel like they've failed and that they've let people down. Maybe later they resent giving so much of their childhood, or their mental or physical well-being, to something that didn't give them what they were promised, or were led to believe they deserved, in return. These athletes can become angry, bitter, and resentful—and who can blame them? They won't get those years back. Chasing the dream can cause real emotional, physical, and mental damage.

For a select few, the dream does become a reality, but the numbers suggest that it's a long shot. And while these odds are not insurmountable, it's safe to say that they are small. So, again, if we come back to the significant costs to participate in competitive sports and the number of years invested, how do we define or determine sports value? Let alone calculate the return on investment? I don't profess to have all the answers, but this book gives the process of sporting excellence a defined structure. It provides a principle-based framework which, in turn, can help you either improve in sports yourself, become significantly more effective at coaching sports, or more objectively evaluate the sports services you are paying for.

There is, without question, significant and real value in sports beyond the outcomes. Sports are a wonderful social activity. You can develop lifelong friendships through sports and build a great sense of community. There are also significant physical and mental health benefits derived from playing sports. But I believe that sports' biggest value is as a mechanism for teaching life skills and lessons. The parallels between the pursuit of excellence in sports and that same pursuit in life are incredibly strong. Sports can teach people the value of hard work and perseverance, communication, teamwork, leadership, how to compete, emotional control, managing success, and managing failure. In addition, you can make mistakes in sports and learn from them without incurring the same level of collateral damage you might have to face in the "real world."

The benefits of physical activity are well documented, and yet so much of the marketing around sports these days is geared toward getting people to sit on their couch and watch other athletes compete. What if those people got off their couches and competed themselves? I think there's room, and maybe even a need, for both. Being a fan and being an active participant do not have to be mutually exclusive activities. For example, instead of playing sports in the world of fantasy, why not benefit physically, mentally, and emotionally from playing sports in the world of reality? Instead of buying your favorite team's latest game jersey, why not use that money to enroll in your local league and compete? Why not have your name, instead of someone else's, on the back of your shirt? People should consider investing in themselves before they choose to invest their time and money in someone else.

Sports are also a profoundly satisfying pleasure. In addition to the pursuit of greatness, the opportunity to compete, the camaraderie of teams, and the opportunity to learn life lessons, sports are also enjoyable and fun. One of the most gratifying aspects of sports is working toward a goal and achieving it. It affords us the chance to become the best we can be at something, and to do that we need to apply principles—facts based in scientific rigor—to our methods of training. These principle-based methods give our athletes the best possible chance of achieving their sporting goals through the process of competitive excellence.

When searching for principles in this pursuit, you cannot look past the work of the late Anders Ericsson, the world's pre-eminent scholar on expertise. I met Anders at a United States Olympic Committee (USOC; now the USOPC, with the integration of the Paralympics) conference many years ago and we became fast friends. His groundbreaking research in expertise became more well-known and accepted through the mainstream use of the term "deliberate practice," which describes a type of practice that is intensely focused on the process of improvement. The use of his research in sports, which Anders and I discussed often, was yet another iteration of how the concepts of deliberate practice and his principles on expertise could be applied.

Most of Anders's initial research in expertise involved people learning skills in activities such as music and memorization. In these experiments, the learners practiced with focus and intent, worked hard, and received expert coaching. Subsequently their skills and level of expertise in their chosen activity improved. The cause-effect relationship between deliberate practice and improved performance was real.

If you work hard to memorize sequences of random numbers and, through your focused efforts and the help of an expert coach, you formulate new mental strategies to achieve that, you will benefit directly from your efforts. You will improve, and it's likely you will get closer to, or even achieve, the memorization outcome goal you have set for yourself. In sports, however, the application of these deliberate practice principles does not yield the same strong relationship between the work and the outcome.

In individual sports, the challenge is quite different. For example, if the goal is to win a 100-meter sprint, you can train as hard as you possibly can, but there's absolutely no guarantee that you'll win. You could false start and be disqualified, you might trip, you might be feeling sick or tired or anxious, or your opponent might beat you—they might be better than you on the day, or on every day!

In team sports, the relationship between the work and the outcome is even less clearly defined. You might be the first person to practice and the last person to leave every day, working as hard as you possibly can, but that doesn't mean that your team will win. And while that kind of work ethic probably helps your chances of playing, it certainly does not guarantee it. So why do all of that work in the first place?

My discussions with Anders over the years were centered around this very question. If deliberate practice is the optimal process for developing expertise, then how do you develop a method and a culture that will support the significant physical, mental, and emotional efforts that are required to achieve significant outcomes in sports? Especially when we can't guarantee the outcomes or even the opportunity to compete? This book will attempt to answer those very questions.

Without getting too far ahead of ourselves, the answer lies in focused and intentional best effort, doing the best that you can in everything you do. This notion of best effort is somewhat counter to our current social climate. Our world of comparison is increasingly fixated on outcomes—especially on winning. So much so, it seems, that anything less is often quickly dismissed as failure. In light of this focus on results, when people don't get the outcomes they want, they tend to stop participating in sports for fear of looking foolish or seeming insufficient. It's as though doing your absolute best and finishing second is somehow an embarrassment or a disgrace. That doesn't sit well with me. Sports should be a lifelong endeavor for all the physical, mental, and social benefits that we've described. As much as we all want to win, we can't all win all of the time. So there has to be more to it.

If you choose to compete you have to accept that, at some point, you're probably going to lose. It's an occupational hazard. But what you do with those losses matters. You can throw a little tantrum, maybe play the blame game to make sure it wasn't your fault, or perhaps have a pity party for yourself. Or you can take 100 percent responsibility for your performance, learn from the experience, and be better the next time you compete. You get to choose. But I think committing to the process of competitive excellence, where you work as hard as you can, learn and make change, compete to the best of your ability, and try to bring out the best in those around you, is a much healthier, beneficial, and enjoyable way to do it.

This process of competitive excellence is most efficient and effective when it is facilitated by a coach. I discuss the concept of "the game teaching the game" later in the book, but there is no question that learning is usually accelerated by a teacher—and coaches should primarily be teachers. Anders used the term "expert coach" in his model for deliberate practice, but this book is not just for experts, so for our discussion we will define a coach as anyone that is a credible source of relevant knowledge and information, who uses principle-based methods in their coaching and teaching, has personal integrity, character, and the right motives for helping their athletes.

Coaching can be a challenging and consuming profession. It is as much a lifestyle as it is a job, and there is a great responsibility that comes with it: helping people. There also seems to be a certain mystique around coaching, a belief that there is some "magic" to the profession that almost deifies successful coaches and normalizes their methods, be they positive and uplifting (think John Wooden), or negative and damaging (unfortunately, there are countless examples of this type of coach). I have said that sports are a great way to teach life, and it's this dual responsibility that coaches should embrace. They should adopt a holistic approach to excellence, and this should be an accepted and expected part of the coaching profession.

Maybe, for professional athletes and those competing in major international competitions such as the Olympic Games, the World Championships, or the World Cup, it should be win-at-all-costs. But even then, I think there are many examples of athletes or teams whose singular focus on outcome has not only left them short of their outcome goal, it has also inflicted significant collateral damage on their athletes as well. There is no magic to achievement. There's just hard work using efficient and effective methods, and the real power of these principle-based methods is that they work. They will make you better.

Having experienced the pursuit of excellence as an athlete and as a coach, I have a cognitive understanding and empathy for both sides of this process. For the athlete, being able to embrace the process of change is a critical part of achievement, but it's very challenging. Learning to deal with failure, to see outcomes as information instead of value statements, is hard. We all want to be good, and feeling like you're going backward, even with the promise of a better tomorrow, requires trust, belief, and patience. Learning to come to practice with an intention and a plan to make change, and then applying those lessons in the moment of competition is the key.

Coaches need to understand that we won't always have five-star talent, but they can make up some, or all, of that difference by being five-star teachers. Coaches coach on the weekends, formulating game plans and tactics, calling timeouts, and making substitutions, but for the other five days of the week, they should be teachers. So, while the athletes have a responsibility to work, learn, and compete, the coaches must learn how to teach, coach, and mentor. If you had to choose one skill to be best at, choose teaching. In my experience, if you do the teaching right, the other stuff tends to take care of itself.

I believe that the teaching component of coaching presents the biggest opportunity for improvement. Science has shown that the correlation between an athlete's initial ability and their final ability is actually very low. In a 2009 study, Anders came to the same conclusion: "First and foremost, it is very difficult to predict which individuals will attain expert levels of achievement."[3] So it's not how an athlete starts their career in sport, it's how they finish. And it will be their capacity for work and for learning, facilitated by a coach, combined with whatever natural talents and abilities they possess, that will have the biggest impact on how good they become.

To further illustrate this point, we should reference the work done by educational researcher Benjamin Bloom, who wanted to find out how the top performers in music, sculpting, sports, mathematics, and science managed to be so successful in their chosen fields. He and his colleagues selected a group of 120 talented young subjects and studied them to learn how talent might be cultivated in people.

His team interviewed these high-achieving individuals as well as their parents, and in some cases, they talked with their coaches and teachers as well. They focused on similarities within the person's field of expertise, and then analyzed their findings across these fields. What they found was really interesting:

> The child who "made it" was not always the one who was considered to be the most "talented." Many parents described another one of their children as having more "natural ability." The characteristics that distinguished the high achiever in the field from his or her siblings, most parents said, was a willingness to work and a desire to excel. Persistence, competitiveness, and eagerness were other often-used terms.[4]

If we accept all of this scientific evidence (and we should!) that says that the "great ones" are not born, they are made—they are talented, hard-working people—then what principles should be guiding the methods we use to help them become great?

Coaches need to be teachers, and we tend to teach the way we were taught. But to teach effectively you need a clearly defined teaching method that is based in scientific rigor—a way that you present and teach the fundamental skills and systems of your sport; a framework that describes an effective pathway for athletes and coaches to achieve significant outcomes through the process of competitive excellence; a method of teaching and learning that, step by step, increases the level of performance and reduces the amount of variance in performance outcomes by controlling the vast number of things you can control. This gives you the best chance of competitive success. There are no shortcuts to greatness, but there are plenty of efficiencies. And that really is how this book is different, we will replace the mystique of tradition with a method that is evidence-based, transferable, and applicable to any age or level.

Talent has been described as either innate or emergent. Innate talents are things you are born with—your height, for example. No matter how hard you try to become taller, it's unlikely you'll have any influence. You will grow to be X'X" tall and that's that. Now, if you happen to be 7' tall, or taller, that innate talent can be extremely lucrative and advantageous —especially if you choose to pursue a career in the NBA. Emergent talents are talents you possess that can change and evolve through intention and effort. My predominantly fast-twitch muscle fiber composition can be developed, with practice and technical training, to allow me to become a world-class sprinter. Basically, the talents you can't change are innate, and the ones you can change or develop are emergent.

Developing your talent, with the hope of achieving a significant outcome, requires commitment. Becoming the best you can be is not for the faint of heart, and excellence is something you earn—it's not given. There are no shortcuts to greatness; there is a lot of hard work, though, and the problem with hard work is that it's easy to talk about but it's hard to do.

The good news is that you can learn to work hard and you can learn how to learn. Working and learning are not innate talents, they are emergent, and as athletes work hard and learn, they tend to become addicted to the process of improvement. As I've said, the great thing about principle-based methods is that they work, and as the athletes work harder, they get better; and as they see that improvement, they want to work even harder, and learn more, and, lo and behold, they get better again. Wash, rinse, and repeat.

This process of incremental improvement is critical because, as you work your way up the food chain in any sport, the ability to execute the fundamental skills of that sport consistently for long periods of time, becomes an important differentiating factor. It's not just physical talent and ability that matters, but also technical mastery and repeatability: good over time is a big part of consistent competitive success. For example, if you're a novice, performing a particular skill at an appropriate level of execution, four times out of five, might help you win your local recreation league. To win an Olympic Gold medal in that sport, you might need to execute that same skill perfectly 99 times out of 100. The difference between these levels of execution and repeatability might seem relatively small, but it's massive. Regardless of the outcome goal, fundamental mastery matters at both levels. Your skill confidence will be connected to your skill competence, which will also be connected to the demands of your competitive environment.

This process of competitive excellence starts with the *what* and the *why*. What are we hoping to achieve? And why are we doing this? Then we move into the *how* with a detailed explanation of a principle-based framework for skill acquisition and skill application. The last part of this process involves bringing all the physical, mental, and social elements that lead to competitive excellence together with the hope of achieving the goal.

Traditional training methods tend to address the components of improvement and achievement separately. We practice to improve technically, train to improve physically, meet with a sports psychologist to improve our mental game, and then work on our team chemistry by doing some "trust falls" (or something similar). While there is nothing inherently wrong with this methodology, I have found that it is not the most effective and efficient path to achievement. I believe that a more holistic approach to competitive excellence creates significant synergies that yield more consistent results and better outcomes. And that's what this book is about: giving this process of sporting achievement a framework that connects the physical (skills/systems acquisition and application), mental (learning/cognitive control), and social (leadership, coaching/teaching, and culture) elements that contribute to the individual and collective pursuit of competitive excellence and significant achievement in sports. If we can operate at the center of all these elements, our chances of success will increase.

But what does operating at the center look like? In 2004, I was an assistant coach with the USA men's volleyball team. We were a good team, and we made a great run in the Athens Olympic Games, but ultimately finished a disappointing fourth place. Now, to be clear, if someone had said we'd make it to the medal round prior to the competition, I think we all would have been stoked. The disappointment stemmed from our inability to seize the opportunity to get on the podium. We didn't play our best in either the semifinal or the bronze-medal match, and being that close to some hardware and coming away empty-handed was really tough.

After Athens, I was encouraged to apply for the USA men's head-coaching job. I'd never been the head coach of any team in the United States, only a professional club team in Europe, so the decision to put my hat in the ring was far from a no-brainer. I took a lot of time to reflect on the current state of the program, formulate a plan, and try to identify the opportunities that could give us the best chance for a podium finish in 2008. One of the things I had learned, coaching in Europe, was the admiration that many people had for the way our American players competed. When you live in the capital of capitalism, you learn about the battle. I had to learn how to compete when I came to the United States, but I also knew about teams from my time in New Zealand and, in particular, how to get people to work together. It became clear to me that, if our ability to compete was a point of differentiation, then combining that with the development of a high-functioning team might evolve into a strong competitive advantage for us. We could possibly "out-team" the rest of the world.

It was not going to be easy, though. There were a lot of things calling for our athletes' attention, and I believed that trying to move from fourth place to somewhere on the podium would require a singularity of focus that we hadn't yet been able to achieve. The national team mattered to our athletes, but so did their professional clubs, who had them for more months of the year than we did. And they weren't teaching our culture, skills, and systems; they were teaching theirs! Building something that commanded the majority of our athletes' volleyball attention was a priority. Remember, most people play a team sport because they want to a part of something bigger than themselves. We had to create an environment that provided and supported that.

The 2004 squad had excellent technical skills and could play great volleyball, but we weren't a completely cohesive squad. It was a group of highly skilled athletes but only a functional team. To become the best we could be, we needed to become a high-functioning team, that is, "a group of goal-focused individuals with specialized expertise and complementary skills who collaborate, innovate, and produce consistently superior results."[5] The 2004 group lacked some of the connections and behaviors that would have allowed them to bring the best out of themselves and their teammates. Using the centered framework, I'd graphically describe the 2004 team like this:

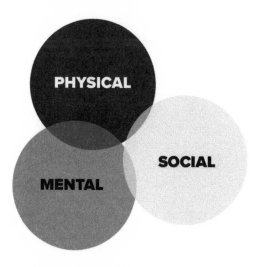

I needed to get a different level of commitment among the team if we were going to have a chance to achieve gold-medal excellence. But to start, there were a few different commitments that I had to make to myself relative to the amount of work required to become the best we could be. Fundamentally, I had to believe that I could be the kind of teacher, coach, and mentor who could help our athletes improve their technical skills and mental mastery, the kind of person who could engender a culture of shared purpose and mutual respect, and the kind of coach who could help them thrive. I had to own all of it.

I also knew that there would be some of turnover within the group, but there wouldn't be a lot because the United States does not have a large men's volleyball talent pool to pull from. I had to figure out, with the athletes we had, how to teach them and how to connect them so they would become a highly skilled, high-functioning team.

By the 2008 Olympics, after a lot of hard work, the technical skills, mental mastery, and culture had come together, and Team USA was operating at the center:

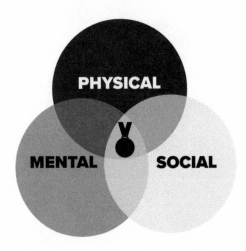

The results speak for themselves. Whether you are an athlete or a coach, you can move the needle from "functional" at your sport to "becoming the best you can be" by applying all the elements of competitive excellence described in this book and learning to operate at the center.

PART I

Foundations

If you want to achieve something significant in sports
you need to start with clarity and conviction, and you
can get that by answering the following two questions:
What is the outcome goal I hope to achieve? and, Why
am I doing this? The *why* is equally as important as the
what because answering both helps you to determine
the *how*. Knowing the desired outcome goal for your
athlete or team and understanding the motives that
are driving that desire allow you to identify the skills
and level of execution required to give you the best
chance of achieving that goal. They help you to identify
competitive advantages and focus your approach to
developing and executing the necessary championship
behaviors.

1

Championship Goal-Setting

The idea of goals and goal-setting is not new, but I can absolutely attest to its immense power and value. There is also a significant amount of empirical evidence to support the impact of goal-setting on achievement. In the mid-1960s, Edwin Locke and Judith Bryan instructed two groups of test subjects to either "do your best" at an assigned task or set goals for their performance prior to attempting the task and going from there. Without exception, the goal-setting group outperformed the "do your best" participants.[6]

There are lots of ways to formulate goals, but a simple and effective construct is the S.M.A.R.T model for goal-setting, which states that goals should be Specific, Measurable, Achievable, Realistic, and Time-bound (meaning there is a clearly defined time frame for achievement). In order to maximize your chances of achievement, your goals should satisfy each of these criteria.

Knowing where you are headed and what you have to do to get there is vital in helping individuals and teams commit to the process of competitive excellence. Goal clarity is critical to goal achievement, and to that end, there are three main types of goals that we must define and commit to—outcome goals, task goals, and daily goals. If championship results require championship behaviors, then we need to set championship goals as well.

OUTCOME GOALS

Joseph Campbell (author of *The Hero with a Thousand Faces*) said, "The privilege of a lifetime is being who you are." These words really resonate with me, and I've shared this quote many times. You are the only *you* that's ever going to be, so if this is your only spin on the rock, why not dream some big dreams and go for it? I am convinced that we are all capable of doing more than we think we can. We only know who we are, and this process speaks to who we dare to become. The outcome goal should be significant—something beyond your current abilities—and your goal statement should clearly and accurately describe what you hope to achieve.

I say hope, because there are only "so many" variables in the competitive equation that we can control. According to the 18th-century English poet Alexander Pope, hope springs eternal—but in the shadows of hope lurk fear and potential disappointment. Even though our path to achievement will likely be challenging, we have to keep those fears at bay and fight to keep hope alive because it's our hope that will get us through the inevitable tough times.

In 2005 we agreed that the goal of the USA men's volleyball team was to become champions of the 2008 Olympic Games in Beijing. That was a huge goal for us, and it was absolutely on the edge of achievable and realistic. While it was unlikely that we would become Olympic champions, it was not impossible. In college sports, the outcome goal might be becoming the best in the conference or the country. For a high school team, perhaps it's being the best in the state. For an intramural team, it might be winning the championship T-shirt. Outcome goals can be adjusted to scale, but again, they have to be based in reality, or perhaps possibility, and they have to be achievable.

The other consideration at this stage is identifying your competitive advantage. What makes you or your team different? Everyone wants to win the championship, so what skill or ability do you have, or can acquire or develop, that will differentiate you from everyone else? What is the main "string to your bow," and can it truly help you separate yourself from the pack and achieve your outcome goal? A big part of belief is connected to identifying your competitive advantage and playing to that strength.

The most common goal in sport is the *W*—the win—and I get that. State champions, national champions, world champions, Olympic champions—everyone wants to win, but not everyone is prepared to do what it takes to maximize their chances of winning. For people who coach for a living, winning and job security go hand in hand; and for anyone coaching in professional sports, that's pretty much their job description—win. I certainly prefer winning over losing, but I think you do yourself and your athletes a significant disservice by defining success solely on outcomes. I currently coach college volleyball, and I believe we have a responsibility to define our program's success in a more holistic way. I don't think we should only be about winning, I think we should be about competitive excellence, so our goal is to become the best we can be with the hope of winning. We should absolutely try to win every time we step onto the court, but we should also be committed to academic excellence and we should invest in our student-athletes' personal development as well.

Winning is great, and it absolutely beats the alternative, but it can also mask a lot of problems. People's attention and introspection are not nearly the same after a win as they are after a loss. You can miss critical opportunities for learning and development when you win. Also, if you play in an average league, to win it you only need to be better than average. I don't like the idea of committing my life to the pursuit of being better than average; I prefer the pursuit of excellence. When you commit to excellence, and take full responsibility for that process and the outcomes that go with it, you are choosing to define who you are. When you let the outcomes define you, you're allowing your opponent to define you. You work to be good enough to beat them; they set your competitive standard, instead of you working to become the best you can be. It's a very limiting way to train and compete.

My mother would say to me, "If you don't have a dream, you'll never have one come true." She was paraphrasing the lyrics from a song in the Rodgers and Hammerstein musical *South Pacific*. Regardless of the genesis of the statement, she was right. We should all dream a little, or maybe a lot! Remember, though, that it has to be your dream, not what someone else is dreaming for you.

TASK GOALS AND DAILY GOALS

The process of achievement will take time and a lot of hard work, and that's where the task goals and the daily goals come in. Task goals are skill- or system-centered. An example might be improving your free throws in basketball or learning to play zone defense. Task goals take time to achieve and usually involve a number of clearly defined steps. Daily goals are how learner intent is established and expressed in this process of achievement. They are the skills, or parts of a skill, you will work on today to improve or acquire the task goals. Going back to free throws, we might be focusing on our foot position or our follow-through or even our pre-shot routine.

Goal setting has also been shown in multiple studies to benefit the performance and learning of motor skills.[7] When determining your task goals and daily goals, you should take a more pragmatic approach. You should move on from what you hope to achieve and start dealing in the absolutes of what you have to do to achieve it.

In *The Seven Habits of Highly Effective People*, Stephen Covey uses the metaphor of the big rocks, little rocks, and sand as an illustration of a time-management strategy. I think it's also a great metaphor for identifying and prioritizing task goals. If the task goals are the big rocks, what are the big rocks needed to achieve the outcome goal? And at what level of execution do we need to perform those big-rock skills? We also want to know which of those big rocks we should work on first. Once we have identified the big rocks, and the order in which we should work on them, we can get to work on determining the little rocks and the sand, and prioritize their achievement accordingly.

To determine these big-rock parameters, we should use statistical analysis. If we consider winning the Olympic Games in volleyball as an example, we should first find out which skills correlate most highly to winning in Olympic volleyball. This is critical because it tells us what aspects of the game we need to work on first and/or most, the core skills that will give us the best chance to be successful. For example, if serving correlates highly to winning but blocking doesn't, we should focus our time and energy on getting our serving skills to the appropriate level and not spend too much time on our blocking until our serving is in place.

It's a bit like establishing Maslow's hierarchy of volleyball needs, but instead of building our foundation on physiology, safety, and belonging, we're using serving, passing, and siding-out. Again, by looking at what the best teams in your competitive environment are doing, using a quantitative measure of performance in these big-rock skills, we can determine the level of execution required to achieve the outcome goal which, in turn, will help us determine and define the necessary task and daily goals.

THE CHAMPIONSHIP MODEL FOR GOAL-SETTING

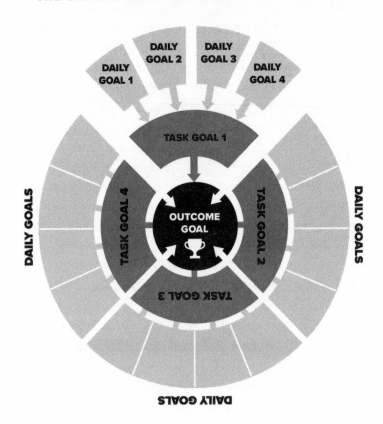

2

Motivation, Motives, and Mindsets

MOTIVATION

There are many types of motivation, but the two most common in coaching are intrinsic and extrinsic. Intrinsic motivation involves performing a task because it's personally rewarding to you. Extrinsic motivation involves performing a task or behavior because of external factors such as avoiding a punishment or receiving a reward. While both types of motivation are important, they can have different effects on the athlete.

Extrinsic motivation can be beneficial in some cases. Working toward gaining a reward, or avoiding a punishment of some kind, can be helpful when you need to complete a challenging task. For example, the last person to complete these sprints has to run more sprints; the first person to complete them gets $100. Intrinsic motivation is typically a more effective long-term method for achieving goals and completing tasks because it makes the athlete feel personally fulfilled. Extrinsic motivation can be helpful in certain situations, but it can also lead to burnout and lose effectiveness over time.

We cover coaching motives in this chapter, but the reason coaches should be motivated to coach is to help an athlete, or a group of athletes, become the best they can be with the hope of achieving something significant. In addition, having the chance to compete can also be a motivating factor. However, if you don't enjoy competition, coaching is probably not the job for you.

For the athletes, the *why* certainly matters as well. While learning, the goal process is critical, but athletes also need to understand how the changes they are being asked to make will benefit them and/or their team. This helps them "push through" the inevitable tough times by establishing a connection between the learning process and the outcome goal. When competing, athletes are usually motivated by elements of the contest itself. The hope to win, the coaches and the other athletes, the crowd, and even the opponents can all act as strong intrinsic and extrinsic motivators.

In terms of the day to day, practices can be motivating based on the types of drills and activities the coach plans. Coaches should find ways to catch their athletes doing it right as often as possible. Praise is more effective for reinforcing behavior than punishment, so I would recommend that you stay away from negative consequences such as running lines or doing push-ups. As an aside, I've known athletes that have developed a strong aversion to physical activities such as running, because of the physical punishments they received and endured while playing competitive sports.

A 2020 study in elementary education showed that teacher praise was an effective way to increase on-task behavior in the classroom.[8] The study found that the more teachers praised the students for doing tasks well, or doing them as instructed, and the less they punished or reprimanded them, the more their students paid attention in class. Students who received the most praise were shown to focus on their work 20 to 30 percent longer than their lesser praised peers.

Positive reinforcement is a much more effective tool for change, but again, you have to operate in truth. You can't tell someone they're doing it right if they're not. You'll lose credibility, and your future attempts to praise good outcomes or good process will ring hollow. That being said, it is clear that you should try to catch them doing it right as often as possible.

MOTIVES

What's driving your pursuit of achievement and excellence? Why invest the most precious resource you have, namely your life, in this endeavor? If you're an athlete, defining your motives matters. When it comes to the *why*, knowing how challenging this process can be, I believe that significant achievement requires your head and your heart. You should be playing a sport that you like and love because, without that, you won't be able to sustain the work required for significant achievement. You should play lots of different sports until you find the one that's right for you. You'll know when it's right; it will become consuming and, like many things in life, if you don't know, you know. Not knowing is a sign that it's not the right sport. The other question for the athlete is: who are you doing this for? Hopefully, the answer is you. You can't succeed with someone else's head and heart. It has to be yours.

If you're leading the effort, your motives will absolutely shape how you teach and coach. When you step into a coaching role, there will be a large amount of power and control that automatically comes with that position. The problem is, though, that this power and control is given, it's not earned. Consequently, by their nature, these positions of authority can attract people who aren't leading for all of the the right reasons.

The temptation of power is real, especially when the barriers to gaining that influence are relatively low, and the potential social and financial rewards can be high. People coach for any number of reasons, but reasons to watch out for include things such as financial gain, seeking personal validation or recognition through the athletes' successes, the opportunity to achieve some unresolved personal sporting aspiration, a strong desire to be the center of attention and control, or possibly being afforded a level of social interaction they wouldn't otherwise have access to. Your motives in coaching matter. The main reason you should coach is to help teach, coach, and mentor your athletes to become the best they can be, with the hope of achieving something significant.

Authenticity is an important part of this process. The principles and methods described in this book need to be expressed through you, not you trying to be someone else. You'll be most effective with your voice, your style, your personality—and you have to own all of it. Take 100 percent responsibility for those in your charge as well as the process and the outcomes. Shakespeare said it best—"To thine own self be true"—and while you might be able to fool some people pretending to be someone you're not, any spaces between your words and your actions will be revealed soon enough, and they'll diminish the buy-in from those you lead.

There is another fundamental question that also needs to be answered: are you the coach, or are you someone who coaches? In other words, is this who you are, or is this just what you do? If you define yourself by your athletes' or team's competitive outcomes, the ego inevitably gets involved—to the detriment of those you lead. Their wins become your wins; they validate you and your coaching acumen. The losses become a personal affront and a source of embarrassment or humiliation. Suddenly, it's all about you, and it becomes a case of "win at all costs." Your athletes become a competitive commodity, a means to your competitive end as you succumb to this insatiable need to win. It's a slippery slope.

Hopefully, you can coach with a healthier perspective than the one I've just described. Hopefully, you are defined by your actions and the significant relationships in your life, not the achievements of your athletes. Your role as coach is something you care deeply about, and do to the best of your ability, but it doesn't define you. You're not on the roller coaster of having your self-worth determined by your vocational outcomes. Instead, you understand that you are a service provider, and the service you provide is to help those under your charge become the best they can be with the hope of achieving something significant.

To have any chance of achieving these significant outcomes, you'll need your head and your heart aligned and invested in the process. The problem with investing your heart is that it might get hurt or even broken. And it is that heartache or heartbreak that often prevents people from going all in. What they don't understand is that they will never become the best they can be without it. They have to accept that the emotional pain of failure is an important part of the learning process. People who try to avoid that discomfort might live a safe life, but they'll never live a full one.

Other people may inspire you—but don't coach or play for them, or to try to prove them wrong (or right!). Fear, anger, and insecurity seldom lead to happiness, let alone greatness. I have often seen this troublesome path of "playing for others" start at the youth sports level. It seems increasingly common for parents to be heavily involved in their children's lives and, in particular, their sport. The parents take them to every practice and attend every contest, and suddenly, they are inextricably connected to the child's activity. They become overly involved, even intrusive, and often they'll feel the need to protect their children, and maybe themselves, from the pain or disappointment that can come with competitive sports.

We shouldn't shy away from these moments of difficulty. There is opportunity in adversity, and these moments present wonderful opportunities for learning and growth. Let your athletes work through that discomfort. It's much easier to learn how to manage adversity in sports than it is to learn about adversity in life, and if our children never get into trouble, they'll never learn how to get out of it.

If the parents aren't insulating them from failure, they might be trying to live their own unrealized sporting dreams and aspirations. But, regardless of the motive, certain patterns of behavior from parents in youth sports seem to complicate things for their children. Young people are impressionable, and parents should be mindful of the type of impressions they are making. In youth sports, especially at the younger ages, celebrating outcomes over effort or process, yelling at children for poor performances, at officials for bad calls, or at coaches for "bad" team outcomes or coaching decisions all make bad impressions.

If I'm a seven-year-old playing a sport, and my parents cheer when I score or win, but say nothing when I miss or lose (or even worse, they yell at me or throw their hands up in exasperation, or some other demonstrative action conveying their disappointment), do I know that my parents value me for me? Or do they only value me for my outcomes? Suddenly, more scoring and winning means more positive affirmation and less negativity, so I quickly want to get better for, or because of, them. My parents are happier when I perform well. My parents' happiness is my responsibility, and so on. You can see how it can all spiral downward from there, and just to be clear, the parents' happiness is their responsibility, not their child's.

Through this cycle of questionable parental influence, the child can become emotionally compromised. They are now playing for parental affection and validation, or worse—to not get yelled at, instead of playing for their own development, enjoyment, and fun. We should love our children for who they are, not just for what they do or the reflected glory we can attain through their efforts and achievements.

Anyone who has achieved anything significant in sports will tell you that becoming the best you can be is difficult. It takes an extraordinary amount of discipline and effort. Do it for you—no one else—because when you make the decision to go all in on excellence, you'll need all of the strength, belief, and conviction you can muster.

You need the dream, the goal, but belief is also an essential part of achievement; its power is real. As Henry Ford said, "There are two types of people in the world, those that think they can, and the those that think they can't, and both are right." I also have found that in sports and in life, if you can't believe in yourself, it's very hard to get anyone else to believe in you. Make sure you're committing to excellence for all of the right reasons; if the motives aren't right, you'll lack conviction and you won't last.

MINDSETS

The question becomes: how do you know if your motives are right? That is, how do you know if you're doing this for the right reasons? One of the main litmus tests is your response to failure. When you perceive failure as an opportunity for improvement, it's probably a sign that you're on a good path: you see your shortcomings as valuable feedback in your process of improvement and achievement. If you perceive failure as an embarrassment or a personal affront, then you should probably look more closely at why you are engaged in the activity.

When people are learning and making change, there's a strong chance that their level of performance will temporarily decline before it improves, and not everyone is comfortable getting a little bit worse to get a whole lot better. Athletes who are defined by their outcomes, whose self-worth is connected to their performance, are seldom willing to be vulnerable enough to make the mistakes needed to facilitate change. The coach's job is to create an environment where it's safe to make mistakes and also to help athletes understand the significant benefits of the changes they are being asked to make. If the athlete believes the change will help them (and/or the team), they will be more likely to engage and do the work, but another important influencing factor in this process is the athlete's own perception of learning and change.

Psychologist Carol Dweck has provided significant empirical evidence that addresses this phenomenon—that how we perceive cognitive ability actually influences our cognitive ability. That is to say, the way a learner perceives their ability to learn, and the learning process itself, influences their capacity for learning and change. She uses the term "mindset" to describe this idea and, in her 2007 book *Mindset: The New Psychology of Success*, she discusses two types: "growth mindset" for those who believe they can learn and change, and "fixed mindset" for those who think they can't. Her research in this area is enlightening and powerful.

To summarize the two perspectives, we should start with the important distinctions between them. Growth-mindset people believe that intelligence can be developed, like muscular strength or cardiovascular fitness. The more you work and stress these systems, the stronger and more efficient they become. Fixed-mindset people believe that intelligence is unitary and fixed. You are born with a certain amount of intelligence, and that amount doesn't change. Dweck then goes on to describe the way each mindset deals with adversity and the different ways they engage in those difficult moments. Growth-mindset people see challenge as opportunity; they embrace it. Fixed-mindset people avoid challenges for fear of coming up short. When things get tough, growth-mindset people lean in to the obstacles they face. They persist and, as Winston Churchill famously told his countryman, "never, never, never, give up." Fixed-mindset people tend to give up rather quickly: when the going gets tough, they quit. When it comes to hard work, growth-mindset learners see the effort as a necessary and integral part of the learning process. Not surprisingly, fixed-mindset learners see hard work as hard, unenjoyable, and are therefore less inclined to do it. When it comes to feedback, growth-mindset learners want it, actively seek it, and learn from it—both positive and negative. Fixed-mindset learners love the positive feedback, but any criticism, constructive or otherwise, is quickly dismissed as a personal affront and ignored. When the two types of learners see their peers succeed, growth-mindset learners celebrate the successes of others. They are inspired by their achievements and work to replicate similar outcomes. Fixed-mindset learners see the success of others as a threat, something that amplifies or draws attention to their own shortcomings or inefficiencies. Consequently, growth-mindset learners tend to achieve at a level at or even beyond that which they aspired to; whereas fixed-mindset learners tend to plateau and give up, never reaching their true potential. Clearly, the pursuit of significant achievement and competitive excellence is better served by a growth mindset than a fixed one.

Even with the right motives and the right mindset, there are no guarantees you'll achieve your goal. What happens if you go "all in" on achievement and come up short? No one likes to look or feel foolish or insufficient, and consequently many people do not commit to the pursuit of significant outcomes in order to avoid those feelings of shame or inadequacy. Fear of failure is real, and it's incredibly limiting. The life of constant comparison that our society currently embraces can amplify our insecurities and make the fear of failure stifling. We should focus on what we can control and what we can achieve instead of looking at what others have done, and somehow let that dictate our actions. Don't compare—become.

People might become risk averse and be reluctant to try something new for fear of embarrassment, but as coaches we have to create an environment that's safe for our athletes, not just physically, but mentally and emotionally as well. A space where people can be vulnerable enough to make mistakes and feel supported and informed enough to learn from them. There is no shame in coming up short in the pursuit of excellence. In fact, those "failures" are a critical part of the learning process.

As unpopular and unpleasant as failure is these days (just look at all of the "epic fails" on YouTube), it is critical in the path to competitive excellence. Often, coming up short will push you to extend yourself and improve your technical skills or other aspects of your performance. You will learn to become comfortable being uncomfortable. In fact, how you frame failure is essential to determining your next steps forward. Just because you fail, that doesn't mean you're a failure, and just because you lose, it doesn't make you a loser. Mistakes happen, but they should not be seen as defining moments. They are simply experiences resulting in information and feedback that can lead to significant learning and growth.

Interview with Daly Santana

In 2015, Daly Santana became a first-team All-American and the Big Ten Conference Player of the Year while playing volleyball at the University of Minnesota. She then went on to represent Puerto Rico at the 2016 Olympic Games in Rio de Janeiro, Brazil, and has been playing the sport professionally in Europe and Asia since graduating in 2015. She was not predicted to have this level of competitive success as a freshman. In fact, she struggled for many years to reach her potential. It's those struggles, those moments of failure and adversity, that she believes shaped her career the most.

———————

When you came to Minnesota, I think it's safe to say that it was not comfortable. It was not easy for you coming from Puerto Rico to the great North. Eventually, you were able to use those moments of adversity to your advantage, even though for a long time it felt like you were fighting them. Would you agree?

Daly Santana: I remember being scared. Everything seemed different from the Puerto Rican culture, even the way we played volleyball—everything I thought I knew was different. To me it was a little bit of a shock, and I thought, Okay, how can I deal with this, how can I change? How can I shift my understanding of this process? But I felt like I really didn't know much about how I should do that. I was absorbing new information nearly every day; it was a lot. By my senior year, I finally felt like, Hey, I can do something with this sense of failure, put it to work, use it rather than just give in to it. I can lean into it.

To make matters worse, in 2014—your junior year—you injured your knee. So injury became part of your adversity as well. Any thoughts on that?

DS: I remember having some conversations with myself about it. I said, "There are two ways we can go about this. We can discover what's going on and try to fix it, or we can just back out and be done." So I think for me at that moment, I needed to make a decision on how to go through the recovery process. It was uncomfortable—a failure in a way—but it was important in my career to make that first decision to be tough and get through it because it helped me with everything that happened after that.

The injury was a part of your growth, but I had no idea at the time that it was kind of a make-or-break moment.

DS: I had to make a big decision—to go through this rehab and recovery process and say, "I want to do it this way." After that big decision, it was easier to make decisions about the little stuff. I started saying out loud what I wanted to do. Things like, "This practice isn't going well. I don't like playing like this, I don't really want to do this, but I'm going to do it. I'm going to work hard, do it the way I've been asked, and try and get better." That's what helped me get through those moments of being uncomfortable, and I learned how to use that discomfort to help me get better.

So let's go through that 2014 season. We lost a few more matches than we had in the past, which was tough. It was a challenging year. But then we had a pretty remarkable turnaround in 2015—which, in large part, was due to you. We ended up winning the conference and went on to the Final Four.

DS: Twenty fourteen was a tough year. We were inconsistent and we didn't qualify for the NCAA tournament—the first time in 10 or 15 years or something. But, because we were hosting the NCAA regional tournament at Minnesota, we had to go watch the games even though we weren't in them. You made us go and watch, and watching versus playing was not enjoyable at all. I didn't really know how to be there.

I guess I just wanted the team to see what we were missing. I wanted it to become personal because we had the talent and ability; we just had to make some changes.

DS: I think that helped me get through our failures. That mentality of committing to improvement, giving 100 percent in the small tasks on my daily routines or practice, even if it's not working out right away. Staying with it, staying in the process.

I had to ask myself tough questions. What if I do the work the way I'm asked to do it? What if I get it? What if I make the change and get better? I already knew the answer to what would happen if I didn't do it, so the question had to be, "What if I do?" It became part of my mentality. If I'm able to do things and improve the way I work, I'll become the version of myself that I want to become.

You were starting to give 100 percent of what you had in all of those moments. And all of a sudden, you're having a good year. But tell me about how coming into 2015, that last year, having faced lots of adversity—dealing with injury, dealing with not making the tournament, being inconsistent in our performance—how did all that change you?

DS: I think before that last year, I was working from a place of fear, the fear of being uncomfortable. And then once I started trying these little things—asking myself, "What if I do it?"—I started to try stuff. Try it, and if it works out or it doesn't, either way it helps you not to stay in the same place. You're building up your mentality and ultimately your game. And I think that process is what helped me develop more of a fearless mentality: just go out and try. I worked on my fear and found a way to move past it and move ahead. I realized, this is it. This is the moment when I have no choice but to become someone other than who I am right now in order to succeed at the tasks and challenges presented before me. It was at that point that everything felt the heaviest. I thought to myself, *I have no idea how to do this, but I most definitely have to take this step.* I didn't know what direction exactly, but I had to try. Then I quickly found that, once you step out of that comfort zone and out of the undecided mentality, then you start becoming better at trying new things. It becomes easier to be focused in your approach to learning new techniques and mastering them. Slowly but surely, as you do the work and learn from the failures, the fear disappears.

So those failures led to growth and change?

DS: Yeah. They teach you which way to go. For example, if I had chosen to stay in the same place and not try to hit a different shot, I wouldn't have become the player I am today. I chose to add to my offensive toolkit [more variety to her attacking], and it changed my career; it changed my life.

Yes, when you came in, you were a bit of a one-trick pony. You had a world-class arm, you could hit it really hard, but when you first came to Minnesota, you could only hit it really hard in one direction. And when people figured that out, there wasn't much else there. You had to change to succeed.

DS: I think a big part of trying new things was also the trust in you, trusting 100 percent in the steps of the process you outlined and the feedback. I began to trust that you could see something I needed to learn. That trust helped me open up and just try new things 100 percent. Not just when it was going great and everything was easy, but all the time. I didn't know how to navigate that uncertainty at first. I didn't want to fail. So I'd hit my "safe" shot instead of the right one.

Also, in the summer before the 2015 season, you introduced the idea of the female warrior to us. That we could be both women and warriors, competitors, even though we didn't feel like society really supported us in that. We needed to let go of that fear and insecurity and just become what we wanted our team to become. The video was our way of expressing that.*

Your strength of character showed in so many ways, like becoming the captain in 2015. You stood up and said, "I'm taking this on. This is who we're going to be this season!" It was pretty amazing to watch you do that.

DS: I didn't want to repeat the previous year. We couldn't afford to repeat certain behaviors or the same mentality as the previous years. I wanted it to be different. Some of our conversations were about leading by example; someone had to step up. I decided we had to do it right. Somebody had to get in everyone's face and push them to change, which I think I did a lot. When it comes from a coach, you kind of expect that, but when it comes from another player, then you're creating your own story within the team and you start pushing each other as teammates. Suddenly, we feel like we're in it together and we're supporting each other, and then there's a snowball effect. All of us were moving toward the same goal.

What you did was a scary thing. I remember we were talking about how leadership can be kind of an island, especially when you go it alone. You took a stand. You were able to hold the team to a new standard because you lived the standard. And you got the team on board: They bought in.

---

* *Gopher Volleyball's Female Warrior*
(https://www.youtube.com/watch?v=b9HT1aXvvlE)

DS: It wasn't easy. I don't think it was pleasant. It was not comfortable.

But you did a great job.

DS: I kept telling myself, "I'm gonna push myself to do this." Even if I wasn't comfortable, or even when I was scared—which was a bunch of times—I just developed this mindset. I believed it was the right way to go. Of course, it was easier once we started winning.

You cared enough to do the right thing and to hold people to the right standards. You started out as a talented but one-dimensional player and became the complete package. You could play the whole game; you could do everything at a really good level and you still had a great arm—and this leadership piece in place as well. It's a powerful example of how adversity can be an opportunity when you approach it the right way. When you see failure as feedback, not as a defining moment.

DS: I agree. Failure can push you—and which direction it pushes you depends on you. It all depends on how you see failure and how you choose to use it.

What I learned has definitely helped my professional career. I feel I now have the tools to be able to meet those moments of adversity head on. Being curious about how to do things better has fueled a lot of that. It's better than being afraid. There is no daily or weekly limit on failure, and each failure is an opportunity to grow and to redirect myself. The rewards are life-changing.

3

Leadership

There are many definitions of leadership, but I really like this one by author and Korn Ferry executive Kevin Cashman: "Leadership is authentic influence that creates value." It's simple and it's true. If that authentic influence gets expressed through one person in a traditional model of leadership, great; if it's better expressed with a leadership group, that's fine too. I believe that coaches have a responsibility to develop leaders, and while not everyone has to become the leader, everyone can, at some point, lead.

Coaches have another fundamental question they need to answer: Should I lead by rule? Or should I lead by empowerment? Regardless of the path you choose, you will always need a few rules, but if you choose to lead exclusively by rule, you'll need to create a lot of rules and you'll create a lot of rule followers. People who end up doing what they are told because that is all that is expected of them, to simply obey in order to avoid a consequence or a punishment. They are seldom choosing the required behavior because it's the right thing to do—even if it is.

Leading by empowerment means fewer rules but significantly more behavioral expectations. If you give people the freedom to do the right thing, they will either choose to do it or they won't. However, regardless of their choice, they have to take responsibility for that choice and the subsequent consequences. As the leader, you will need to establish the behavioral expectations and provide guidance, but ultimately it's up to those you lead to make the right decision at the right time. There will undoubtedly be some mistakes, and consequently some lessons learned, but this ability to make the right choice at the right time consistently, in sports and in life, will improve—and I don't think there's anything bad that can come from that.

We also know that one of the few constants in life is change, and so it is with teams. Leading and building high-functioning athletes and teams is not algorithmic. The same inputs seldom lead to the same outputs year to year, or even day to day, because the people and the competitive environments are constantly changing. The challenge is figuring out how to apply your guiding principles to the athletes in a way that works best for them—the talents, skills, and personalities unique to that athlete or group. Once you've figured out what's optimal for this campaign or season, you'll likely have to apply those same principles differently for the next one. The principles don't change, but their application does, and while the desired picture of what we want the team to achieve might stay the same—the athletes smiling, holding the big trophy—the pieces of the puzzle and the way they fit together are always different. The leader must adapt and adjust, and then help the athletes adapt and adjust, to ensure a consistent level of success.

As the coach, you'll need to the lead the team, and your knowledge and consistency will be critical to your success. You'll also need to develop internal leadership—the athletes need to lead as well. Traditional models of team leadership assign (usually by player vote or coach selection) a captain to lead, but I've found that the mechanism for team leadership can be expressed in different ways. I've worked with teams that have had great captains. Their leadership has been incredibly impactful and influential. But on some teams we've had equally effective co-captains, and on others we've had a leadership group and no captain at all. Like all things in coaching, you need to do what's best for your athletes. Determine the best leadership model for your group, based on the personalities and emotional range of the people in it. Do not feel constrained by tradition or expectation. Create the internal leadership model that you think will give the team the best chance of achieving its goal.

Having coached both men and women during my career, I am often asked about the differences between the two. The most important thing to understand is that there are way more similarities than there are differences. Before we are women or men we are people, and if you treat people with genuine care and concern, and respect them and invest in their development, things generally work out fine. In addition, volleyball is one of the few sports that tries to adjust for the difference in height and power between women and men by having a different net height for each gender. With the USA men, we had athletes who could jump and touch over 12' playing on a net that's about 8' high. They jumped high and they hit the ball hard. Some of our USA women were jump-touching over 11' and played on a 7'4" net—they could jump high and hit it hard too! Women, like men, have human bodies that are prone to the effects of gravity and the laws of physics, so the way we trained and the way we played were very similar.

When I decided to coach the USA women in 2009, after coaching the USA men in Beijing in 2008, it was seen, at the time, to be an unorthodox career move, as I had never coached a women's team before. Whatever the perception was, I felt that given we had achieved all that we had set out to do with the USA men, the idea of spending another four years reinventing that same wheel was not very exciting for me. More interesting, though, was the idea of taking a body of knowledge that had been developed over many decades with the USA men and applying that to the USA women. Fortunately, USA volleyball agreed and supported the change.

When my hiring was announced, I received a number of congratulatory calls from my coaching peers, and I also received a few words of "warning" about the differences I would encounter and the limitations I would now have to deal with. "The women won't be able to do this technique," or, "They can't play this type of system." It was surprising and a little disappointing. I like to live in the world of possibility, not the world of limitation. I was excited to see what could happen if we took the principles and methods we used so successfully on the men's side and applied them to this new and incredibly talented population.

It turned out that, while there were lots of similarities between the teams, there were also some differences. I am not an expert on gender difference in sports, but generally it was clear that the main spaces were in communication and connection. For example, in a timeout, if we needed to play better defense and I was addressing the team about their overall lack of defensive effort, a male player would hear me and would likely think that I was talking about another player on the team. If I was saying that to a female team in a timeout, an athlete could be more likely to think that I was talking directly to her. The guys generally started from a place of ego and bravado, where you had to chip through the armor to get them to be vulnerable enough to listen and make change. The women were generally starting from a position of doubt and insecurity, you had to help them understand how good they really were, and go from there.

In light of these doubts and insecurities that are present in, but are by no means restricted to, our female athletes, we have to acknowledge that some coaches will try to leverage those fears to their own personal advantage. We need to address leadership by manipulation and fear. Unfortunately, it's more prevalent in sports than we'd like to admit, and while it can yield significant outcomes, the collateral damage to the athletes is often significant as well. A life in fear can never be a life in full. Fear is the curse, and yet it is often used to manipulate athletes' behavior.

Fear-based coaching can be manifested in a couple of different ways. The first is, as we said, someone preying on the fears and insecurities of those they coach to their own personal advantage. Second, and perhaps more insidious, is the very real phenomenon of fear-based coaching arising from the coach's own fear of being found out. That is, people finding out that they don't really know what they're doing. As we've stated, the coaching profession lacks rigor relative to academic preparation, and it automatically gives the underqualified coach significant power and authority. So there are coaches who are given this influence over the people they coach, who feel or, even worse, know that they lack the required relevant knowledge and information to do the job effectively. They become so afraid that people will "find them out" that they push those personal fears and insecurities onto those they coach. Things suddenly become very authoritarian. These coaches micromanage and speak to things already known (think lots of team rules and a focus on outcomes or coaching to the last play instead of the next one), but there is no substantive teaching or coaching around athlete development or team culture. There's lots of skill repetition in planned and very controlled environments, but there's not much skill instruction. There's no clearly defined skill constructs and minimal technical feedback. The coach will yell and belittle an athlete about the last play—"How could you miss that shot?"—but they won't do anything to help the athlete or the team to answer that question.

There's hierarchy, deflection, lots of meetings behind closed doors, silos within the team and staff, and even though it might seem like there's structure, there's a feeling of unease and discord that comes from the credibility gap created by the excessive attention to detail in some parts of the program, and the complete absence of structure or relevant knowledge in others. For example, we've learned how to run after mistakes as well as anyone in the country, but we were never taught how to correct the mistakes we're running for. Add to that the lack of authentic connection and communication, and it makes for a challenging environment for everyone.

Human beings are neurologically wired to respond to fear. Fight-or-flight responses are real; consequently, fear pushes people out of rational thought and into the space of emotional response. They act out of fear/worry/concern over the possible outcome or consequence. Coaches who lead with fear ultimately hurt the people they coach. It is a selfish and careless way to lead, and the constant stress and resulting anxiety can be crippling for their athletes.

If we look outside of sport, at our current social climate, we can see how our society is influenced by fear. We have all succumbed to the constant "doom-scrolling" our news feed offers us and the subsequent emotions our devices and their content creates. We're hooked! The headlines and articles, even the refresh function, are all designed to evoke an emotional response and keep us coming back for another dopamine or adrenaline hit. For example, with a focus on FOMO—"fear of missing out"—we're flooded with images of other people living their "best" lives and engaging in their "best" activities.

We can't compete, let alone keep up. There's also FOPO—the "fear of other people's opinions," that is, letting other people's thoughts and opinions dictate our actions and behaviors for fear of being judged or, even worse, canceled. There's also the fear of things like the end of the world, the virus, political extremism, geopolitical unrest, the stock market crashing, violent crime, and so much more. The number of things we are "forced" to care about, the number of things demanding our attention, seems to never end. It's exhausting.

Becoming the best you can be is a daunting task that will force you to grow and evolve in countless ways. During that process, there will be doubts, fears, and insecurities you will have to learn to overcome. These are barriers, both real and perceived, that you'll have to push through along the way.

Doubt kills the soul, and in your personal pursuit of competitive excellence, or if you are leading others, there will be moments of doubt, moments when you'll question what you're doing or how you're doing it. We know the power of belief, and it's so important that you believe in yourself and your methods when these moments arise. To keep these doubts at bay, I recommend that you develop an attitude of belligerent optimism—that is, the ability to have resolute conviction in your abilities when facing the inevitable moments of adversity that will come your way.

Belligerent optimism and belief are not arrogance; they are connected to confidence. Arrogance is an exaggerated estimation of your current abilities, while confidence comes from your belief in those abilities. It's a much different place to operate from. While none of us have all of the answers to the difficult questions competitive excellence presents, those who operate from a position of belligerent optimism believe they can and will figure them out and find the next step forward in their pursuit of excellence.

We don't have to be afraid. We can respond to that neuro-logical response, and we don't have to lead with fear, either. Creating environments that are safe and free from negativ-ity, that allow the athletes to learn and evolve without fear or manipulation, leads to better learning and better performance. As the coach, you are not the puppet-master Geppetto pulling your athletes' emotional strings. You are there to help, support, teach, coach, mentor, and consistently operate in truth from a position of genuine care and concern for those you lead.

4

Work

Working is engaging in a mental or physical activity in order to achieve a result. If we are going to achieve something significant, we will need to do a significant amount of work. Hard work is hard, it is difficult, but it's also an essential part of competitive excellence and significant achievement.

Los Angeles Rams wide receiver Cooper Kupp is a great example of someone whose work ethic has allowed him to achieve something significant. Certainly, his final ability seems to have surpassed people's estimations of his initial ability. Out of high school, Kupp's chances of reaching the NFL seemed bleak—in fact, his chances of playing college football weren't great, either. On a scale of one to five stars, five being the best, Cooper Kupp was evaluated as a zero-star college recruit. When he played his last high school game in 2011, not a single university had offered him a football scholarship. Finally, the zero-star, zero-offer recruit received two offers, and Kupp chose to play at Eastern Washington University, where he got to work and changed his stars. The head football coach at EWU said he'd never seen an athlete with Kupp's work ethic. "He didn't waste a minute, ever. I know a lot of people say it, but he truly wasn't going to let anyone outwork him."[9]

The work paid off. Kupp finished his collegiate career with an NCAA record 6,464 receiving yards. He also set FCS (the NCAA Football Championship Subdivision) records for receptions (428) and receiving touchdowns (73). He was also a third-round NFL Draft pick in 2017. But he wasn't done yet. Kupp had a remarkable 2021 season, in which he earned NFL Offensive Player of the Year, was named a first-team All-Pro—by unanimous decision—and won a Super Bowl ring. From zero to hero.

Hard work does not make talent irrelevant—it cannot replace it—but it does allow that talent to reach its full potential. Dr. Piers Steel, a professor of procrastination—yes, there is such a thing—at the University of Calgary, has an astute observation about people who rise to the top of their field:

> People who are exceptionally talented are . . . exceptionally rare. But from what we know about the prevalence of procrastination, people who work hard are also pretty rare too. Most of the time, you are going to end up competing against rivals with one of these attributes, talent or hard work, not both. Those with natural aptitude and the willingness to put in the effort are as rare as diamonds and twice as valuable.[10]

Hard work is important, but as with all things in life, you can have too much of a good thing. To guard against doing too much work, you should learn to work smart as well. Mental and physical burnout are real risks for athletes at any age, but our younger athletes are especially vulnerable to this affliction. They blindly put their faith in their coaches and do what they are told no matter what. But young athletes are often not physically ready to assume the training loads that some youth sports programs demand. We all understand and accept the injury risk that comes with physical activity, but excessive training volume and/or intensity can lead to significant injures from fatigue and overtraining.

The issue of early specialization is also a contributing factor in burnout. Young athletes who only move their bodies in a restricted number of movement patterns for prolonged periods of time are more prone to overuse injuries. These young athletes who play only one sport are not only prone to physical injury, they can suffer from mental burnout as well. They get sick of playing the same sport all of the time and stop because they become bored and never really wanted to do it anyway—their friends played, or their parents pushed, but either way it didn't make for an enjoyable experience.

As the physical, mental, and emotional demands of their sport and their lives increase, older athletes can also become susceptible to burnout. More is not necessarily more when it comes to training. Overtraining can result in decreases in performance, enjoyment, and cognitive function as well as changes in emotion and physiological effects such as loss of appetite or a compromised immune system. Rest and recovery are essential to keep our athletes healthy and engaged. Hard work is one thing, but we also need to be smart, otherwise the demands being placed on that athlete will push them to stop.

Coaches have to be aware of burnout as well. I'm often asked about work-life balance, and I reply that I don't think there is a universal formula for it. Certainly, coaching is not a balanced profession, it's not 9:00 to 5:00, it's 24/7, so I suggest that you evaluate your work-life balance by the strength of the significant relationships in your life. If they are healthy and strong, you're probably good. If those relationships are strained or compromised, then you probably have some work to do. As an aside, I think that one of the most important significant relationships in your life is your relationship with you. In addition to all of the other people you have to help and take care of, you also need to help and take care of yourself.

As for the job, it can be consuming. There is always something you can work on because becoming the best you can be is a never-ending process. It's a pursuit, not a destination, so being able to separate you (the person) from you (the coach) is important. Your personal commitments need to be a priority in addition to your coaching commitments. To maintain a healthy balance, you will need support and perspective.

PART II

Development

The path to achievement in sports, particularly as it relates to coaching and skill development, needs clearer definition. Many have suggested that playing the game is the most direct route to expertise. But is playing the game the best way to teach the game? The answer is, "It depends." For young athletes who don't have access to youth, AAU, or club sports with private lessons and personal trainers, and who view sports as a way to change their stars—their life's circumstance— playing the game has repeatedly been shown to be a great way to learn and improve. Experience is a wonderful teacher—the best, in fact, particularly when the student is committed to improvement.

In contrast, there are also people who have played a particular sport for years and years and have shown little or no improvement. These people are playing just to play, to have fun, to work out, or for social interaction. There is little intention or drive to improve, and consequently they don't. If sports could provide a tangible path to the dream of a better life, though, the intention to learn and improve would be palpable.

If you add effective coaching and teaching methods to that intention and drive, you'll now have purposeful practices facilitated by a coach who can guide the athlete's development. So, if the goal is to become functional at a sporting activity, the formula for that process could be:

Competitive Competence = Sport-like Practice + Learner Intent + Teaching/Coaching

If the athlete has physical talents and abilities that lend themselves to being successful in the sport, then competitive excellence and significant achievement become a possibility. The formula now becomes:

Competitive Excellence = Talent + Sport-like Practice + Learner Intent + Teaching/Coaching

If these are the building blocks for competitive excellence, what does the building process look like? To start, let's clarify what the primary responsibilities are for each stakeholder in this pursuit of significant achievement. For the athlete, for anything significant to occur, they have to work, learn, and compete. For the coach, to facilitate that significant outcome, they have to teach, coach, and mentor their athletes.

Determining the principles that will guide the athlete's development on this path to significant achievement is critical. A principle is defined as a fundamental truth that serves as the foundation for a system of belief or behavior. The benefit of guiding principles is that they serve as wonderfully rigorous evaluative criteria with which to determine your methods. There are lots of ways to teach, coach, and mentor. Undoubtedly, some are more effective than others, but without guiding principles, it's hard to separate the wheat from the chaff.

5

Research in Learning and Skill Development

In the 1980s, motor learning professor and renowned volley-ball coach Carl McGown codified research in the science of motor learning and applied it to coaching volleyball. After being coached by Carl in college, and then coaching with him for a number of years, I could see that, over time, some spaces grew between his framework and the emerging science on skill acquisition and skill application. Over the years of my coaching career, and the application of this emergent research to my coaching methods, I arrived at the following Championship Model, which I believe better describes the principles and behaviors that drive this process. In order to better understand the Championship Model, I think it's important to understand the research that supports it.

In 1967, psychologists Paul M. Fitts and Michael Posner created a model to describe the three progressive stages of learning. These stages were described as cognitive ("what to do"), associative ("how to do it"), and autonomous ("doing it").[11] In the cognitive stage, the skill to be learned is identified, as are the component parts of the skill; the athlete is forming a schema, a mental representation of what the task demands. In the associative stage, the athlete links the parts of the skill into some kind of whole-task attempt, that is then followed by feedback and practice. Finally, in the autonomous stage the learned skill becomes automatic; there is no conscious thought or attention while performing the skill—the athlete just does it. When an athlete gets to the autonomous stage, they have acquired the ability to execute the skill and apply it to different conditions within the competitive environment; they are unconsciously skilled.

PHASES OF SKILL ACQUISITION

(Fitts & Posner, 1967)

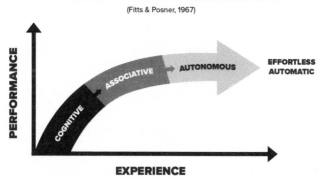

In 1972, Dr. Ann Gentile published "A Working Model of Skill Acquisition with Application to Teaching."[12] Her research was notable because it was one of the first attempts to scientifically connect motor learning and skill acquisition to teaching. Gentile's work also contrasted the different characteristics of open- and closed-loop motor skills (open-loop = an uncontrolled environment, such as hitting a pitched baseball; closed-loop = a controlled environment, such as hitting a baseball off a tee) and connected their acquisition and subsequent execution to teaching and learning strategies. She proposed a two-stage model:

- Stage 1, "Getting the idea of the movement": the learner attempts to determine the general motor pattern of the skill that will produce the desired outcome.
- Stage 2, "The diversification phase": the learner works to acquire the required level of skill execution by refining the motor pattern learned in Stage 1.

Gentile recognized the need to connect motor learning research to a working model of skill acquisition and saw her study, not only as a practical means to this end, but also as a starting point for further research in this area.

A year later (1973), John E. Nixon and Lawrence F. Locke published "Research on Teaching in Physical Education" in the educational textbook *Second Handbook of Research in Teaching*.[13] They built on Gentile's model to describe and emphasize the concurrent responsibilities of the teacher and the learner in the skill-acquisition process. Their framework provides the basis for the Championship Model.

In 1975, Richard Schmidt proposed the schema theory for motor control, suggesting that motor programs contained general rules that can be applied to different environments or situations. The term *schema* comes from the field of cognitive psychology and is defined as a pattern of thought or behavior that organizes categories of information and the relationships among them. In other words, a mental representation of a task or a thing. In Schmidt's theory, the schema contains generalized rules that generate the commands to produce a specified movement. When learning a new movement, an individual may generate a new motor pattern based on the selection of parameters (features of a movement, such as the speed or force required), or refine and apply an existing motor pattern depending on the learner's previous experience with the movement.

An example of this scaling of motor schema would be throwing a ball in different directions or distances. As people practice throwing the ball in different directions or distances, they learn the relationship between the parameters and the different performance outcomes. This information is collected in two schemas: the first is named *recall schema*, which connects outcomes to parameters. The second is *recognition schema*, which connects the expected sensory consequences of a movement to the movement's outcome. Think of it as recall schema initiating and controlling the movement, and recognition schema evaluating and storing it for future use. Schmidt suggested that there are four pieces of information that get stored after a movement:

1. The environmental conditions as the movement begins;
2. The specific requirements of the movement (for example, speed, or force);
3. The sensory consequence of the movement (that is, how it feels); and
4. The outcome of the movement.[14]

Schmidt's work in this area was significant. His idea that generalized motor programs could be modified and applied to various movements was a critical step forward in the application of motor learning theory to sports skill learning.

K. Anders Ericsson was the world's preeminent expert on the study of expertise. His concept of deliberate practice has been widely applied in many domains, but its role in sports, especially team sports, has not been clearly defined. Ericsson was a prolific researcher, and his work in expertise represented another significant step forward in the processes of skill acquisition and achievement. *Peak*, the 2016 book he coauthored with Robert Poole, details his research and findings in this area.

In terms of applying his research to sports, there are a couple of his studies that are of particular importance. In 1980, while at Carnegie Mellon University, Ericsson and his colleagues published "Acquisition of a Memory Skill."[15] As the title says, the study was about memorization. Psychologist George Miller's famous 1956 research on short-term memory suggested that we can store and recall, on average, five to nine pieces of information in the short-term memory structures in our brains. The purpose of the study Ericsson and his colleagues undertook was to see if the subject, an "undergraduate student with average memory abilities and average intelligence," could expand that short-term memory capacity through regular, intensely focused practice sessions. During each practice session, the subject was presented sequences of random numbers at a rate of one per second. The practice session would last for about an hour because the task was difficult and longer sessions at this level of intense focus were unsustainable; the subject had three to five practice session per week.

After hearing the sequence of random numbers, the subject had to repeat the sequence back. If the sequence was recalled correctly, the next sequence was increased by one digit; if it was recalled incorrectly, then the next sequence was decreased by one digit. The researchers not only wanted to record the subjects' outcomes; they were interested in the subject's process as well. Immediately after half the trials (randomly selected), the subject provided verbal reports of their thoughts during the trial. At the end of each session, the subject was also required to recall as much of the material from the practice session as they could.

Over the course of 20 months of intense practice (264 hours), the subject's ability to remember random number sequences steadily improved from seven to 82 digits. This increase in performance was attributed to strategies the subject devised using *long-term* memory and retrieval methods—mnemonic associations, where additional meaning is assigned to the sequences that need to be recalled. For example, the number sequence *4, 1, 3, 2* could be stored as *four minutes and 13.2 seconds*, a fast time in which to run a mile. Another example in language is the acronym ROYGBIV as a way to remember the colors of the rainbow (red, orange, yellow, green, blue, indigo, violet). The subject's short-term memory ability did not seem to change but compared with other memory specialists, the subjects' acquired skill in memorization was now at an expert level. This study showed the positive effects of intense, focused practice on skill acquisition and application.

In a subsequent study, the subject from the initial study became the coach, and they coached a new subject in the same skill of remembering sequences of random numbers. The coaching helped, especially in the early stages of learning where, over the first three days of practice, the new subject increased their recall capacity from 10 digits to 19. After 286 hours of training, the new subject could recall 68 numbers, and after 800 hours of training that number increased to 104.

The first of these two studies described the parts of the deliberate practice process. The subject had a specific goal, there was immediate feedback on each attempt, and the goal was adjusted depending on the outcome of each attempt. The work was challenging; it was difficult and uncomfortable and required the learner to augment their understanding of the task first by describing their process, the kinds of mental representations the subject was creating to remember the number sequences; and secondly, by testing for retention at the end of each practice session, not just recall.

The subject would plateau at times, making little or no progress. After the initial experience of frustration, they would create new (new to the subject) ways of improvement leading to a subsequent breakthrough and improved performance.

The second study addressed the value an expert coach could bring to the skill-acquisition process. Between the two studies, a framework for deliberate practice was created: start with a specific goal, and have regular short sessions of intentional/ challenging/uncomfortable practice with expert coaching and feedback.

In 1993, Ericsson and his colleagues published "The Role of Deliberate Practice in the Acquisition of Expert Performance,"[16] which describes two studies that were conducted in the field of music. One tested violinists of different abilities, the other tested subjects with differing abilities on the piano. These studies looked at the effects of deliberate practice over time. They suggested that, while deliberate practice was an important part of the skill acquisition/application process, the amount of time spent in deliberate practice activities was also a significant differentiating factor. They argued that the differences between expert performers and average performers were directly related, not to a difference of innate talent, but to the amount of deliberate practice they had completed. They suggested that expert performers had completed a decade or more of focused and intense practice to improve their performance to an expert level. This process of improvement was facilitated by an optimal distribution of deliberate practice over the course of that time.

This finding gave rise to the now infamous, though somewhat inaccurate, 10 years/10,000 hours rule that became popular through Malcolm Gladwell's 2008 book *Outliers*. I say inaccurate because this "rule" reduced attaining expertise in a particular field to a set quantity of deliberate practice, and yet it is clear that different tasks require different amounts of time to master. For example, it only took the subject in Ericsson's 1980 study 264 hours to reach an expert level in memorization. It also didn't take into account other critical elements such as the quality of the practice activities the learner engaged in or the quality of the coaching they received.

Consequently, the formula for deliberate practice relative to achieving expertise could be expressed as: defining a specific goal, regular short sessions of intentional/challenging/uncomfortable practice, expert coaching and feedback, and doing these activities for a sustained period of time. It is also important to recognize, at this stage, that innate physical talent does play a significant role in this equation when we apply deliberate practice to sports. For example, the number of under-6' tall athletes in the NBA is low, as is the number of 7' tall gymnasts.

The activities in these experiments were closed-loop in nature. That is to say, the environments were controlled, there were no random variables, and consequently the learner was able to see a clear relationship between their efforts and their improvement. The harder the individuals worked, the more they focused, the better coaching they received, the better outcomes they achieved, the closer they came to expertise.

In 2002, Dr. Gabriele Wulf published "Enhancing the Learning of Sports Skills through External-Focus Feedback," in which she studied attentional focus and feedback as they related to motor skill learning.[17] Her research found that a significant improvement in both skill learning and retention resulted from having the athlete focus on external cues (described as the effects of the movement, such as shooting a basketball while focusing on making the ball contact the rim of the basket) instead of internal cues (described as the parts of the body, or sequence of parts, that were responsible for the movement, such as shooting a basketball while focusing on the amount of flexion in your wrist). In addition, she also found that athletes who learned using external cues (keys and feedback) were able to show improvement under different feedback conditions. That is to say, you could provide feedback for the athlete on every attempt, or every third attempt, and a similar level of learning occurred. In comparison, the athletes that learned using internal cues were adversely affected by more feedback; the more often they received feedback, the less learning seemed to occur. This finding was contrary to the generally accepted idea that more feedback led to more learning. The way the feedback was framed and phrased seemed to be the differentiating factor.

Lastly, it's important to remember that the body cannot do anything without the brain telling it to, so the execution of these motor skills is as much contingent on the strength of the neural pathways controlling them as it is on the muscles performing them. When learning or modifying skills, a fundamental question to consider is this: are we changing an old habit, or are we building a new one? Research, such as that documented by author Daniel Coyle in *The Talent Code*, has shown that building new habits, though initially more difficult, is a more efficient path to fundamental skill acquisition and mastery than changing old habits. Habits are neural pathways that are created by an antecedent and a subsequent response, followed by some type of reinforcement. The neural pathway is strengthened by the myelination of the neurons that facilitate the response (think antecedent hits the brain, brain sends the signal via myelinated neurons, neurons fire the muscles to do the task, and get the reinforcement). These neural pathways are built and strengthened through this myelination process. The more the neural pathway is used, the more myelin is wrapped around the neurons—and the faster and stronger the signal and the subsequent habit it produces becomes. These neural pathways get built through the process of myelination—but they don't get unbuilt. The strength of signal might fade over time if the pathway is not used, but the pathway itself cannot change. Consequently, it is more efficient and effective to build and myelinate a new pathway instead of trying to change an established one.

Before we move on to the model, I understand and acknowledge that there are other ways of approaching skill-acquisition and motor-program development. Research has produced other motor-learning constructs such as Bernstein's Dynamic systems theory and Newell's model of constraints. In this book, I am describing the research and principles that have been effective in my coaching career, but in no way is this book the definitive tome on motor-learning theory. You should feel free to review other research in this area and determine the principles and methods that will work best for you.

6

The Championship Model for Skill Acquisition and Application

	1 →	**2** →	**3**
ATHLETE RESPONSIBILITIES	• Set goals • Identify skill • Set learning intent	• Formulate skill schema	• Attempt skill
COACH RESPONSIBILITIES	• Set goals • Create motor programs + skill constructs • Demonstrate skill	• Develop motor program	• Optimize response
GUIDING PRINCIPLES AND BEHAVIORS	• Goal presentations • Information processing • Demonstrations • Keys • External cues • Teaching method • Learner intent	• Specifity vs. generality • Transfer • Whole vs. part practice • State-dependent remembering • Blocked vs. random practice • Progressions	• Practice environment • Practice • Opportunities to respond • Massed vs. distributed practice • Drill constructs • Fatigue • Mental engagement

4	5	6	7
Process feedback	• Modify or repeat goal/schema steps (using 1, 2) • Identify changes for next skill attempt	• Repeat skill attempt (using 3, 4, 5) *or* • Attempt skill application (7)	• Apply skill • Set and enact competitive intent • Compensate and adjust
Give initial and augmented feedback	• Help determine appropriate skill modification or progression (using 1, 2)	• Repeat skill teaching (using 3, 4, 5) *or* • Move to skill coaching (7)	• Systems and tactics pre-/during competition • Coach the athlete • Review
Feedback Teach to the relevant key Goals for drills Competition Testing Data	• Refer to goal and skill schema columns (1, 2)	• Utilize all previous skill acquisition principles/ behaviors *or* • Move to skill application principles/ behaviors (7)	• Specialization • Emotional control • Decision-making • Best effort • Mental focus

Based on the model developed by Nixon and Locke (1973)

COLUMN 1

	1
ATHLETE RESPONSIBILITIES	• Set goals • Identify skill • Set learning intent
COACH RESPONSIBILITIES	• Set goals • Create motor programs + skill constructs • Demonstrate skill
GUIDING PRINCIPLES AND BEHAVIORS	• Goal presentations • Information processing • Demonstrations • Keys • External cues • Teaching method • Learner intent

ATHLETE RESPONSIBILITIES

Athletes have to work, learn, and compete. Framing that process is important. The outcome goal is what we hope to achieve, but the work is centered around the task and daily goals. The skill- or system-centered task goals are achieved through a commitment to achieving the daily goals. Athletes should come to practice having identified what parts of a skill, or skills, they are working on and bring an intention to try to learn and make the required changes. Demonstrations are an important conduit to the skill-identification and schema-creation process, but most athletes watch demonstrations and focus solely on the outcomes. The best learners focus on what the demonstrator is doing to produce those outcomes.

Through this process the athlete can build the layers of mastery required to achieve the task goals. Think of those layers like the rings of a tree: you don't add them all at once. They add up over time. The progress is sequential and incremental—it doesn't happen overnight.

That doesn't preclude making a breakthrough, suddenly having things "click" and making significant improvements in a short period of time. Learning is not linear. You might work to achieve a particular daily goal and, after four days of training, feel as though you have hit a plateau and made no progress. Then suddenly—or actually, not so suddenly—on day five, you get it, something clicks. You achieve the daily goal and then turn that success into a new layer of skill that makes it possible to achieve, or at least make progress toward, the task goal that you are working on.

COACH RESPONSIBILITIES

Coaches must teach, coach, and mentor. If you are going to teach, you have to determine exactly what it is that you're going to teach and then determine how you are going to teach it. To start, you need to identify the skills, behaviors, the systems of play, and the level of execution that correlate most highly to achieving the outcome goal. This is how you determine the task goals and daily goals for your athletes. Next, using your guiding principles, you need to create the motor programs you want your athletes to learn. The skills, the skill constructs, the keys, and all the elements required to teach the skill as effectively and efficiently as possible. Lastly, you should not only tell the athlete what the task or daily goal is, you have to show them as well. Either the coach or another athlete needs to demonstrate the skill so the required skill task is clear.

GUIDING PRINCIPLES AND BEHAVIORS

Goal Presentation

In Part I, we looked at determining what the outcome goals could be. We also introduced the concept that, whether they are individual or team goals, they should be SMART: specific, measurable, attainable, realistic, and time-bound. Setting a goal of becoming the best tennis player in the world when you are operating at a novice level of play is not SMART—the goal doesn't match your reality.

Once the outcome goal has been established, the process of improvement and achievement can begin, and the way you frame the goal, and the subsequent behaviors that support it, matters. The outcome goal must be defined clearly and correctly, but it can be expressed in a number of different ways. In my experience, the following mechanisms allow the goal to be articulated, understood, and committed to most effectively:

- Mission Statements
- Vision Statements
- Behavioral Standards
- Values
- Rules

Mission Statements

To create a meaningful mission statement, you must identify the goal that you hope to achieve and then determine the skills and behaviors required to achieve it. You don't necessarily need specifics regarding the skills and behaviors, you can paint this picture with broad strokes, but the goal has to be clear. Everyone who reads it must know and understand what you hope to achieve and the types of behaviors and behavioral expectations they are committing to. The mission statement invites both intellectual and emotional connection to the goal. It should be shaped by contributions from the people who will be doing the work, which, in turn, will foster a genuine sense of ownership and accountability in everyone.

When I started coaching the USA men's national team in 2005, I thought it was important to frame the quadrennial with a clear goal and a mission statement. Outwardly, it may have seemed a little corny, maybe even hackneyed, but I believed that without a clearly articulated goal and a description of the commensurate behaviors we would need to commit to, we would not move the needle very much.

The first summer after an Olympics is often seen as a bit of a throwaway. In 2005 there were a few major events: World League (now called Volleyball Nations League [VNL], which we were not competing in); the NORCECA zone championships (North America, Central American, and the Caribbean); and an event called the Grand Champions Cup, a six-team tournament held in Japan with the five zone champions (Africa, Asia, South America, NORCECA, and Europe) plus the host country. That summer, there was also an event called the America's Cup (for volleyball, not yachting), involving the best North and South American teams, and that tournament was held in Porto Alegre, Brazil.

One of my main logistical objectives for the team was to move from Colorado Springs to a location at sea level. While the Olympic Training Center had great facilities and support staff, the elevation was a real issue for us. Serving is disproportionately important in volleyball and passing (receiving serve) is critical, too. The ability to execute well in these first-contact skills will often determine the outcome of a match. Colorado Springs is in the alpine desert, at an elevation of around 6,500 feet, and the volleyball travels a lot differently there than it does at sea level. An average jump-spin serve in men's volleyball, with the ball moving around 70 mph, travels about three feet further in Colorado Springs because the air is less dense, meaning that the thin air exerts less pressure on the ball than the denser air at lower elevations, and consequently the ball travels farther.

Every major event of the quadrennial, including the Olympics and the Olympic qualifiers, was being held at sea level. This presented a huge competitive disadvantage for us. USA Volleyball put some feelers out, to see if there were any cities that might be interested in hosting the team, and we received strong interest from the city of Anaheim in Southern California. As part of our due diligence, we trained for two weeks in Anaheim prior to heading to Porto Alegre. By that time, we had most of our guys back in the gym, and because we were all housed at the Anaheim Hilton for two weeks, I decided one day that we'd take an afternoon off from practice and get to work on the mission statement.

We got everyone, both players and staff, in a meeting room and started talking about what our goal should be. In my opinion, the outcome goal for our team had to be to try and win the Olympic Games in Beijing. Culturally, as Team USA, I just felt that we had to set our sights on being champions, regardless of how unlikely that seemed at the time.

I casually mentioned the idea of becoming Olympic champions to the group, and not surprisingly, the idea was met with strong pushback. The thought of becoming Olympic champions was wonderful, but the reality of our circumstance was much different. The Brazilian team, reigning Olympic and world champions, were faster; Russia was taller; Serbia was technically better. All these teams, and about half a dozen more, could possibly win the Olympics in 2008. How dare we say that we wanted to do that, let alone that we would?

Before you can even talk about winning Gold you have to first qualify to go to the Olympics. Of the 222 countries in the world that play volleyball, only 12 get to compete in the Games. In 2004, to qualify for the games in Athens, Team USA beat Cuba three sets to two, winning 15–13 in the fifth set. It was an exhilarating and harrowing experience! The margins between winning and losing at that level are wafer thin and a point here or a point there might result in four years of hard work going down the drain. Because of this, Team USA in 2005 was reluctant to have "Olympic champions" as the goal. However, after more discussion, we finally agreed that as wild, unlikely, and audacious as the goal seemed, it was actually the right one for our team.

After reaching that agreement, we then split into smaller groups, composed of both coaches/staff and players, to discuss what kinds of behaviors we thought we needed to exhibit to give ourselves the best possible chance of achieving the goal.

We reconvened. Each group shared their thoughts and ideas, and I wrote everything on a board for everyone to see. After all the groups had finished speaking, I asked if they would let me take all their content and try to construct a mission statement from their ideas and contributions. They agreed and, after some more thought and wordsmithing, the goal and the mission statement were born. We finalized it over the next few days, and everyone agreed to it and signed off on it before we got on the plane to Brazil.

If you asked any of the guys today, or back then for that matter, they would tell you that putting Olympic champions down on that document was probably a bit of a stretch. History would suggest otherwise, but there were two very important consequences that occurred from openly expressing our goal and committing to it. First, everyone had a say in what we said we were going to do. They had a voice; it was heard, and they were included in the goal setting/mission statement process.

Second, there was an instant accountability mechanism built into our program. If we said that we are trying to become Olympic champions, then we had to act like it. You can't publicly commit to a championship outcome and then act contrary to that without being seen as duplicitous, at the very least.

We went on to beat the 2004 Olympic champions, Brazil (with their same 2004 Olympic lineup), in the final of the America's Cup in five sets. The goal seemed a little more realistic after that.

Here is that Mission Statement:

USA Men's National Volleyball Team
Mission Statement

The mission of the USA Men's Volleyball Team is to become champions of the 2008 Olympic Games in Beijing. As members of this team, we will invest ourselves completely in pursuit of this goal.

We are committed to becoming students of the game. We will work tirelessly with our bodies and minds to realize our individual and collective potential.

We will compete relentlessly, and we will remain composed and focused in the heat of battle.

At all times, we will strive, in thought and in action, to represent ourselves, our team, and our country with honor.

The statement was a constant reminder of whom we hoped to become and what we hoped to achieve. The words became our actions, and by the end of the quadrennial, we had achieved everything that we had written down. It was a powerful and transformational document.

Interview with Reid Priddy

Reid Priddy is a four-time Olympian (2004, 2008, 2012, and 2016) and a two-time Olympic medalist (gold in Beijing and bronze in Rio). He also played on the FIVB and AVP beach volleyball tours.

Do you remember when I introduced the idea of the mission statement to the team?

Reid Priddy: Yeah, I remember it well. All of a sudden, we were in the hotel having a meeting instead of practicing. And not just one meeting—I think there were several—and I just remember thinking, *Shouldn't we be sweating and doing athletic things right now? I don't understand why we're in a room and talking about some journey.* You had thick enough skin to be able to handle the darts that were coming your way in that moment. No one was stoked to be there.

Then we write down that we're going to be Olympic champions in 2008, and we had no business writing that statement. It makes sense after 2008 that we would write that, but in 2005 it made no sense. If the rest of the world would have seen that, they would have laughed at us. We weren't trending, we weren't on the rise, we weren't the next hottest team. Nobody was thinking like, *Oh, you gotta watch out for that USA team.*

Okay, it was a bit of stretch, but I always thought it was the right goal for us. Did it ever make sense?

RP: So we went through the process. We were a part of it, but it wasn't until the gold medal was around my neck that I sort of looked at that mission process as ground zero—I thought, *Now I get it! Now I get why we did that!* Even after the 2005, and 2006,

2007 seasons, I don't think I was cognizant of the fact that starting at the board and ending at the board (where practice was written for the team to see) each day, referencing the mission statement in the beginning and end of practice, helped us to live it. The mission statement sort of became our identity.

Can you tell me more about how you think that happened?

RP: You reinforced the whole thing. And not just you, but your staff as well. We had constant reminders of being in the gym with purpose. We knew—we were clear about our purpose, and everything that we did was sort of in alignment to that one goal, which was to win the Olympic Games in 2008. And so, as I look back on it now, obviously, I see this sort of lifelong dream goal and then these value statements underneath. And it was very powerful. It's been life-shaping.

What did you learn from that mission process?

RP: What was that realization in 2008? What did I learn from that? I would say for a good nine years after, there was this underlying thought that I avoided that said, *Reid, you saw how important that mission was for your professional life. What could that do if you were that clear on your actual life?* I sort of avoided it, and it wasn't until 2018 that I sort of leaned into my personal *why*, and that has unlocked what I'm doing now. And I'm trying to take a page out of that book, I'm trying to draw on that experience. It was a very formative and happy time. It's powerful. We tend to think of this as more of an organizational mechanism, but I do think it's powerful as a personal one as well.

Vision Statements

Vision statements are not centered on a specific goal, and they are not necessarily time-bound like a mission. They speak to something imagined and then guide us to make that something a reality. The vision statement will often appeal to an emotion or an idea, and it uses that to shape future behaviors. Because sports are so outcome-focused, the vision statement in sports is used more to articulate long-term team or program change as opposed to a specific outcome goal. Taking an example from the corporate world, Nike expresses its vision statement as follows: "We see a world where everybody is an athlete—united in the joy of movement. Driven by our passion for sport and our instinct for innovation, we aim to bring inspiration to every athlete in the world and to make sport a daily habit."

In some ways, our outcome goal statement of becoming Olympic champions was also our vision statement. It was certainly alive in our imaginations and spoke volumes about the team we hoped to become. When you have four years together, working daily with the same goal in mind, the mission and the vision might align. When the time frame is shorter, you might need another mechanism to create the connection between your outcome goal and the behaviors required to achieve it.

Behavioral Standards

Not every team has the emotional range or maturity for a mission or a vision statement, and not every team has four years to work and/or will that mission into reality. But, if the coach comes up with a mandatory goal and mission for them, which they had no part in creating or committing to, that's about as powerful as printing a T-shirt stating, "Teamwork Makes the Dream Work" and assuming that wearing it will somehow facilitate goal achievement.

In lieu of a mission or vision statement, you could put behavioral standards in place. You identify the behaviors required for achievement, and then everyone commits to something like, "For the next six weeks, we are all going to do these six things." You might even want to precede it with "For the next week, we're all going to do this one thing," and then grow the practice from there. A great example of an expressed commitment to a set of behavioral standards is the Olympic athlete oath. Each Olympian agrees to the following statement during their Olympic campaign:

> In the name of the athletes, we promise to take part in these Olympic Games, respecting and abiding by the rules and in the spirit of fair play, inclusion and equality. Together we stand in solidarity and commit ourselves to sport without doping, without cheating, without any form of discrimination. We do this for the honor of our teams, in respect for the fundamental principles of Olympism, and to make the world a better place through sport.

The athletes might compete for the full two weeks of Olympic competition; their event could also be over in 10 seconds. No matter how long they are competing, the athletes pledge that they will adopt and abide by these behavioral standards.

Values

Establishing and consistently adhering to a set of behavioral standards may also be a challenge for some groups, but you still need a mechanism to keep the process of goal achievement moving forward. Emphasizing a set of values may be the best way to unify thought and subsequent action about the behaviors required to achieve the goal.

While people might know the dictionary definition of *values* and *behaviors*, do they actually know their meaning? What those behaviors look like in real life? Respect, gratitude, hard work, honesty—athletes might know what the words literally mean. But do they know what it means to live them? The words and the actions should be closely aligned and clear. The space between what the athletes say and what they do needs to be small.

In 2014 we had a young team at the University of Minnesota. They wanted to be good, but for no other reason than their youth and inexperience, they didn't know how to apply or live all the behaviors required to achieve their goals. Instead of a mission statement, we put together a list of our core values and defined what these words meant to us. We made posters listing our values and hung them in the locker room and in our offices, common areas where they'd be seen regularly.

Our 2014 season was challenging. We went 19–11, which is by no means terrible, but we did not qualify for the NCAA tournament. It was the first time the team had not qualified for the dance in 15 years. We got through the season, worked hard that next spring and summer, and went 30–5 in 2015, winning the conference and making it to the NCAA Final Four before losing in the national semifinal. It was quite a ride. We had a mission statement in 2015, and it absolutely helped frame our season, but most importantly, the words in that mission statement had life, they had meaning, and that was a direct result of our 2014 values shown here:

Minnesota Volleyball Values

Hard Work—Giving best effort in everything we do is the cornerstone of our program.

Learning—and the process of mastering the skills and systems of the game.

Competitive Excellence—We say and do everything we can to win every time we step on the court (in practice and in matches).

Attitude and Gratitude—We choose to be positive in all things and appreciate what we have and the people who help us.

Genuine Care and Concern—for our teammates. We are committed to developing and nurturing our relationships.

Toughness—Determination and resilience. We will never give up.

Integrity—We always choose to do the right thing.

Unity—Team first. We look for ways to help the team and the people on it.

Defining these values helped our athletes to live them, and that made all the difference moving forward. Knowing is not enough, you need to understand as well.

Rules

All athletes and teams need rules, but in my experience, the fewer the better—less is definitely more. In *A New Kind of Science*, physicist Stephan Wolfram writes, "Simple rules can produce complex behaviors."[18] I think he's correct, and I think his finding applies in more fields than physics. Conversely, lots of rules produce rule followers, people who just do what they're told for fear of a consequence. There's nothing complex about that.

Fewer rules also give you the freedom to treat situations, and the people in them, the way that they need to be treated.

More rules means less flexibility, and at the end of the day, you want to be able to coach to the situation and not be painted into a corner, where you're forced to do something you'd prefer not to, by Rule 1(C), Section 4(b). Coaches need to be consistent voices of knowledge and empowerment rather than merely reciting and enforcing rules. Through both their actions and their words, they should lead people to choose behaviors that support the goal and its achievement rather than simply sit in judgment and impose consequences.

Even if you have a clearly defined goal and a mission statement in place, rules will help reinforce and encourage the concrete behaviors you want such as, "Be on time," or, "Go to class." Equally, if not more powerfully, though, rules can also address a behavioral expectation: to reference the USA men's mission statement: "At all times we will strive, in thought and in action, to represent ourselves, our team, and our country with honor." When applied in this fashion, the "rule" suddenly covers a large range of behaviors.

On teams, athletes often want a player who violates a team rule to be punished for their actions, but the motivation is usually grounded in such thoughts as, *Why am I following the team rules if they aren't?* or, *Why follow it if there is no consequence for violating it?* I think we should consider reframing team rules as mechanisms that are created to help athletes achieve the common goal—where the consequence for violating the rule is putting themselves and the team at risk of not achieving the goal. That is to say, the rules will help our path to achievement, violating them will hinder our progress. For example, if there's a rule about being on time, and a team member is late, the consequence is really the effect of those lost minutes of practice or lost opportunities to compete. Losing time, in addition to the trust lost with your teammates and coaches, is the consequence—as opposed to a punishment. Instead of demanding justice, teammates should consider a more empathetic approach. For example, why was my teammate late? Do they need help? If so, how can I help them? With the understanding that any rule infraction hurts not just the individual, but the team is well.

Ideally, you want people to choose to do the right thing because it is the right thing to do. The athlete's motivation for complying with a rule should be because it supports the team's goals, not just to avoid the punishment. If the rule or guideline doesn't support the team's goals, then maybe it should be reconsidered.

Information Processing

Although the human brain is complex and has incredible processing power, cognitive researchers have concluded that our brains are constrained when it comes to processing information. Our ability, in this regard, is limited. Researchers have pinpointed bottlenecks in the way we process inputs that impede our ability to process and retain information.[19] As we know, too much information will overload the learner. In addition, talking is not practicing, so choose your words carefully. If you are decreasing practice time and running a risk of overloading the learner by speaking, make sure the words count.

Demonstrations

Words are often inadequate and ineffective at communicating motor skills. Words like *up* or *fast* convey general meaning but do not always accurately convey things like specific body positions or complex movement sequences. Motor learning studies have found that movement information is better retained in memory using observational practice and learning. Seeing the skill successfully demonstrated by a peer, coach, video, or picture gives the athlete a mental model of the desired outcome that they can attempt to imitate.

Coaches should be able to execute the keys presented and their skill constructs correctly, otherwise they cannot demonstrate them. Coaches can be good demonstrators, but I believe that peers are better models of these desired behaviors. For example, in my collegiate coaching, I can demonstrate the skills I am teaching, but I am not an 18–21-year-old female. Having a teammate demonstrate, or showing a video instead of, or in addition to, my demonstrations, seems to be more effective.

Our job as coaches is to connect the athlete to the daily and task goals. Words are often inefficient in this process, but words combined with demonstrations (yours or those of someone who has mastered the desired skill) can help the athlete better understand what's being asked of them and help them to make the required change. Lastly, if you can't demonstrate the skills in your sport, you absolutely need to be able to teach them. Helping the learner attend to the right elements of the demonstration is critical for effective learning.

Keys

You need to create skill constructs for the fundamental skills of your sport—a framework that expresses the most critical elements of the skills by "chunking" information, or breaking it down into small, manageable parts. By "critical elements," I am suggesting that you distill these skills to their purest essence. You want all the parts of the skill that matter for efficient and effective execution, and none of the parts that don't. You want to say a little but mean a lot. Examples could be phrases like, "weight forward," "swing through the ball," or, "arms straight."

These chunks of skill information are called *keys*. Information presented this way can be more easily understood, retained and applied by your athletes, and more efficiently delivered by the coach. Given that our brains have a limited capacity to process information, we should try to have as few keys to our skills as possible. Research on short-term memory suggests that most of us can retain five to nine pieces of information,[20] and given that we should accommodate all our learners, keeping the number of keys to five or fewer for teaching a skill makes a lot of sense.

External Cues

Gabriele Wulf's article, described earlier, was important because it brought to people's attention the importance of athletes' attentional focus (internal or external) relative to learning and suggested how that focus should influence the way we determine and design our keys and feedback. Most research up until this point suggested that the athlete should be guided to the correct movement by feedback and instruction. Many of the discussions were centered around the type of feedback and the frequency with which it was given; athletes' attentional focus was a new and different consideration. Under the guidance hypothesis, the coach would provide the athlete with verbal feedback referring to the part of the skill execution that required the most change or improvement.[21] Often this feedback would refer to an athlete's body part and its position, or several body parts and the sequencing of their movement. The hypothesis was found to have some limitations, especially when feedback was given too frequently.

Wulf began researching the influence of attentional focus and, later, attentional focus in conjunction with feedback frequency. She defined an internal attentional focus as a cue that referred to the athletes' body parts and their movements. An external attentional focus referred to the effect of the athletes' movements on their environment. After training and testing novice and advanced subjects learning a volleyball serve for service accuracy, she found that the group that was being taught using external cues and feedback showed more improvement and better retention than the group being taught with an internal focus.

She then used different feedback schedules for subjects learning a type of lofted soccer kick which was taught, trained, and then tested for accuracy. The groups were taught using either external or internal cues and were given feedback with different frequency. Both groups were divided further into four, and the groups of internal- or external-focus subjects were either given feedback after every practice repetition or every third repetition.

Again, she found that external cues were more effective for learning and retention, but she also found that feedback frequency using internal cues influenced learning. Even though both internal-cue groups performed worse that the external-cue groups, internal-cue subjects who were given feedback on every repetition did not learn as well as the subjects who received feedback on every third repetition. Under this condition, more feedback did not lead to more learning.

The group using external cues learned more effectively than their internal-cue peers, but the frequency of feedback did not produce a significant performance difference between the two groups. More feedback, combined with an external cue, did not seem to impede learning or retention. Both external-cue groups, at 33 percent and 100 percent feedback frequency, performed the skill at a similar level. In fact, the 100 percent group performed slightly better, though the difference was not statistically significant.

So what does all this mean for athletes and coaches? If we're playing golf and thinking about the position and sequencing of our feet, shoulders, arms, and wrists during a putt instead of seeing the hole, establishing a line, and making solid contact, we will likely miss. The internal focus will present opportunities for individual evaluation of each part and possibly lead to excessive self-assessment or negative self-talk during the action, resulting in a poor putt. Focusing on all of the parts of a skill internally leads to what Wulf calls "micro-chokes" at each stage of the action and impedes the execution of the whole skill.

If we are teaching someone how to putt, we should devise skill keys that describe the movement effect of the putting action and refer to external cues, such as the line of the putt or swinging the putter like a pendulum, instead of focusing on all the things we have to do to hit it and get the ball in the hole. Novice learners, who might require more feedback from a coach, will not have their learning inhibited by a higher frequency of feedback when using external cues, and more advanced learners will not have their progress inhibited with less feedback or be overloaded with more. Bottom line: anytime we can coach or teach using an external cue, we should, but we also have to understand and accept that our athletes are using their bodies to move, so it will be difficult to create keys and feedback that are completely devoid of any reference to their bodies.

Teaching Method

To teach effectively, you need to have a clearly defined teaching method—that is, a way you present the skills and systems of your sport—a method that allows you to present your keys and give your athletes opportunities to respond and opportunities for feedback. This is not just a question of key order (that is about progressions), although your keys should be both incremental and sequential. The objective here is optimized learning, but remember, you are trying to help the athlete. Teaching is not just a process of principle application, it's a human exercise that requires not only the communication of relevant knowledge and information, but the support and encouragement of the learner as well.

To start (assuming you know nothing of the learner's skill level), you should demonstrate the task to the learner and then let the learner attempt the task, as demonstrated, without any instruction to assess the learner's abilities. It's important that the coach assess the learner's current ability and teach to that. There is a tendency for coaches to coach to the level they want to coach to but, regardless of your coaching knowledge and acumen, you have to coach to the level of the learner. You have to meet them where they are and work from there.

After that initial assessment, you then demonstrate the whole skill again but focus the learner's attention to the first key. The learner attempts the whole skill again, focusing only on that key while receiving feedback specific to that key only.

Once a sufficient level of proficiency has been shown relative to the first key, the task is demonstrated again with attention directed to the second key. Again, the athlete practices the task with attention on the second key and, if necessary, can attend to the first key as well. You can now teach to both elements, but remember that the human brain has a limited capacity for processing information; the more complexity you add to the task, the harder it will be for the learner's mind to attend to the different parts of it. Make sure the athlete can demonstrate the required level of execution for the current key before you move on to the next one. Once an acceptable level of proficiency has been shown, you can demonstrate the whole skill again, with an emphasis on the third key, and so on, until all of the keys have been covered.

Generally, the drill constructs associated with this phase of learning are simple and constrained. They are about skill acquisition not skill application. Once a sufficient level of skill acquisition has been attained, though, you can start to increase the randomness of the drills, making them more game-like, to increase transfer and start working on and teaching to the application of the skill. For example, in volleyball, if you are learning how to forearm pass, you might start by throwing the ball underhand to the athlete as they try to acquire the fundamental mechanics of the skill. Once they can do that, you then might have the athletes forearm pass in pairs, and from there progress to receiving a ball bowled underhand from the other side of the net. Now the athlete can attend to the skill, but they also get to see the ball coming over the net, as it does in the game, and manipulate their forearm platform to make the ball go to a target that represents the setter, instead of to a partner directly in front of them. Then you might serve an easy topspin serve from halfway into the court so the athlete can get used to tracking the ball off the server's hand, then an easy float serve, and then a regular serve from the base line. Finally, they receive serve with three passers, and you can talk to them about calling for the ball, seam responsibility, and the elements of the application of the forearm passing skill, not just its acquisition.

Here is a summary of the teaching method we have just described:

- Demonstrate the skill.
- Let the learner attempt the skill to evaluate their initial abilities.
- Demonstrate the skill with attention focused on the first key.
- Let the learner practice with feedback given specific to key 1 only.
- Once a sufficient level of mastery has been exhibited, move on to the next key.
- Demonstrate the skill with attention focused on the second key.

- Let the learner practice with feedback given specific to key 2.
- Repeat the process until all of your keys have been covered.

In addition to the teaching method framework, the other aspect of teaching is the teaching itself. The way you deliver the information. Inherent to the success of this process is the athlete trusting the coach. Coaches must ask themselves, "Am I a credible source of relevant knowledge and information?" Assuming the answer is yes, athlete-coach trust can be developed through effective teaching and coaching. An important way to help that process is to help mitigate negativity bias. Helping our athletes learn to assess their outcomes and the subsequent feedback they receive as information, as opposed to a personal indictment, is important. It's simple: the grass is green, the sky is blue, this is what you did. Coaches can also help athletes separate their self-worth from their outcomes—for example, they can tell them that they like them and that they are a good person, but this was the opportunity for improvement that presented itself on that particular repetition. Help them to think the best of themselves because their natural inclination will be to think the worst.

Coaches should strive to be five-star teachers first; the five-star coaching will follow. I tell people often that coaches need to be salespeople before they can become change agents. By that, I mean that, as a coach, before we're going to effect any meaningful change, we have to get buy-in from the athlete; we have to sell it. We must help the athletes understand the value and importance of the changes that we're asking them to make. If the athlete doesn't want to make a change or doesn't see the value in making the change, there won't be much change, and we'll just end up wasting a lot of each other's time and energy.

Now, we aren't selling used cars here, we are "selling" parts of the process of competitive excellence. Things like fundamental skill mastery, repeatability, mental resilience, the ability to read the game, and the importance of playing well with others. These are critical differentiating factors for goal achievement. While an athlete might have talents or abilities that lend themselves to possible success, as that athlete goes further along their competitive path in their sport, any technical inefficiencies will become barriers to their achievement and advancement. At the top levels of competition in any sport, everyone is strong, fast, or superior with regard to whatever physical talents their sport requires for competitive success. The differentiating factor, then, between being good and great in any sport is not talent alone, it's the combination of talent, skill mastery, and skill application.

Future NBA Hall of Famer Steph Curry is a prime example of an athlete who was projected to be good at the game but was not seen as having what it took to become an all-time great in the NBA. Curry has talent, no doubt, but that's not what sets him apart. It's his talent combined with his fundamental skill mastery that makes him different. In 2020, Curry made 105 consecutive three-point shots in practice, breaking his previous record of 77. There is no doubt his fundamental mastery of basketball shooting mechanics combined with his ability to stay focused enough to repeat that skill successfully 105 times makes him unique. Talent plays a part, but that is not the only string to his bow. His talent got him far, but it's his talent combined with his skill that makes him great.

As we've said, the athlete has responsibilities in this process of change, one of which is to learn. A big part of the coach's role in facilitating that process is to develop the mental skill of learning right along with teaching the mechanics of the physical skills.

When it comes to developing an athlete's ability to learn, we need to understand and communicate that there is a difference between traditional perceptions of intelligence (aka "book smarts") and what we're focusing on, which requires sports smarts. Some athletes might believe they are not particularly adept at learning because they didn't get an A in algebra, even though their sports skills and decision-making in the field of play are remarkable. They hear "learning" and tend to recoil. You could tell them that they are smart, and they would quickly tell you that's not the case. They've been conditioned to believe that there is only one measure of intelligence, and that is connected to IQ and academic achievement. There is even the social narrative of the "dumb jock" that we have to battle. Your job as the coach is to help them believe that, not only is intelligence expressed a number of different ways, but they absolutely have the capacity to learn and make change. And then you have to find ways to help them to do that, to connect the content to the learner in a way that works best for that learner.

It's also worth noting that our current educational system relies heavily on digital tools. And certainly, the social interactions of our athletes have an increasingly significant digital component as well. But sport is not digital; it's analog. You cannot tweet or TikTok your way out of trouble in the competitive arena. You can't do an online search and download the skills you need in the moment of competition when you need them. If you want to have the best chance of competitive success, those physical, mental, and social skills have to be taught and learned so they can be applied at the appropriate times.

Another consideration is the style of teaching you choose to implement. There are a lot of teaching styles out there, but for the purposes of this book, I'm going to discuss two: the didactic and Socratic methods of instruction. In didactic instruction, the learner is presented information. That's it—a one-way instructional path whereby the student receives information and instruction from the teacher. In Socratic instruction, the learner is questioned by the teacher about their understanding and experiences. In sport, the coach and the athlete would engage in a dialogue about a practice situation or skill repetition. This process of instruction would usually be initiated by the coach asking questions of the athlete to stimulate critical thinking and promote understanding.

Coaches should apply both methods of instruction to their teaching. For example, at the beginning of practice, when talking about the day's activities or discussing the goals or intention for the day's practice, a didactic approach is probably best—*Here's what we are going to do today*. Didactic instruction should also be applied when you're explaining drills or adjusting a drill during practice. In terms of skill acquisition and application, though, a Socratic method of instruction—asking the athletes why they made that choice or how that repetition felt—can provide both the coach and the athlete greater understanding of the skill requirements and the learning process. The coach gets some insight into the athlete's awareness, not only of skill execution but of skill application as well, and the athlete is pushed to engage in thought about what and why they are doing a particular skill, as opposed to simply doing it without understanding the context of the skill.

Learner Intent

One of the most important additions to the Championship Model, integrated from Ericsson's research on deliberate practice, is learner intent. We have suggested that our coaches become five-star teachers. Concurrently, our athletes need to commit to becoming five-star learners.

Going to practice to sweat is not actually practicing. It's called working out, and you can do that at your local fitness center.

Practicing should be a much different endeavor. Practice should be physically demanding but should also be mentally and, on occasion, emotionally demanding as well. It's much tougher to learn than it is to sweat, but committing to that process is the key. Learner intent makes change more efficient. A decision to commit to the process of mastery, the idea of adding as much value to your sport as you can, involves a tremendous amount of focus and hard work. Learner intent, therefore, becomes the critical differentiator between good performers and great performers—even for athletes with a lot of natural ability.

The athlete should come to practice with an intent to learn and a daily goal in place. That daily goal, or a daily goal per skill, should be shared with the coach so that feedback can be given specific to the task that the athlete is working on. The goal can also be written on a board in practice—a public declaration of their practice intent. Writing things down for others to see also allows for feedback and support to come from your peers, not just your coaches.

In addition to the goal, the athlete has to come to practice with the intention to learn and/or compete, depending on the activity. Athletes are human, and they are prone to all of the frailties of that condition, just like the rest of us. They will often come to practice burdened with the slings and arrows of the day, and they have to learn how to cross the line.

To "cross the line" means that once I start practice, I bring all of my attention, focus, and effort to that practice, regardless of what's happening in the outside world. Obviously, we're not talking about serious issues that should take precedence over practicing; we're talking about the detritus of life like a missed deadline, an argument, someone cutting you off in traffic— anything that can rob you of your focus relative to the task at hand. Cross the line—if you're going to be there, be there, and give the pursuit of excellence the full attention and effort it deserves.

People readily engage in the parts of the work that they are good at and enjoy, but the decision to go all-in on excellence means you will have to change whatever needs to be changed, even when you're not good at it or the work is uncomfortable. You commit to doing everything you can to achieve the outcome goal. There also has to be an understanding and an acceptance of the very real frustration that comes with hitting the inevitable plateaus that come with learning. It's tough not getting better (or getting a little bit worse!), feeling like you can't make the changes you're being asked to. The hard work is difficult, but it's also necessary. You need to get comfortable being uncomfortable.

I tell my athletes that they need to be urgent, patient, and kind with themselves in their pursuit of excellence. They need to remember, as we all do, that they are fallible; they will make mistakes. No one has ever played, or ever will play, the perfect game of volleyball, so I ask them to take perfect outcomes off the table and, instead, I suggest they pursue perfect process. The idea that they can commit to the process of excellence by trying to control things that they can, such as work rate, learner intent, attitude, and so on. This is difficult as well, but you can learn to do it. The world's current narrative around success, as seen through the lens of social media, makes achievement seem easy and so many athletes get frustrated when the reality is different. Life is not "fair" (because fair is subjective), and neither is the pursuit of excellence—but that doesn't mean it's bad.

When learning skills, athletes need to focus on process over outcomes, trusting that the right process will lead to the right outcomes. The temptation of the outcome is real, and athletes, especially in controlled environments, can get away with inefficient mechanics and still get the desired outcomes. You have to commit to the right process even if, in that particular instant, you didn't need to. Just because you can get away with an inefficiency, doesn't mean that you should. In addition, focusing on outcomes can draw attention away from the process. Don't let what you want get in the way of what you have to do to achieve it. Focus on process, focus on excellence, and the results tend to take care of themselves.

The 2022 Winter Olympics were held in Beijing, China. U.S. skier Mikaela Shiffrin speaks to this idea of focusing on good process to facilitate performance outcomes. Shiffrin told reporters that she wasn't thinking about finishing on the podium before her race:

> I'm not focusing on the medal anymore. It's just trying to do my best execution every day. Anyway, that's my best shot at a medal. So it's a little bit of maybe a paradox …that your best chance to have that performance is to stop thinking about the performance and to focus on what you're doing in that moment. So I'm just trying to be present in the moment, especially with the downhill.[22]

Athletes often get frustrated with change. It's hard and it doesn't happen quickly, and because they are living in the world of comparison, they compare their ability to change in sports to their ability to change in other areas of their lives. But what do novice learners in sports know about the timelines for motor skill acquisition? Why compare your ability to row on the crew team to your ability to learn Spanish? These are different processes and different systems, so helping the athlete to accept their journey as it is, free of judgment or comparison, and to stress the value of the focused and intentional moments, practices, weeks, years, and so on, in the process of excellence, is the key.

Much of this process comes down to how you choose to perceive failure. I suggest to our athletes that they should try becoming curious about failure, as opposed to being defined by it. Why does it happen? Why do I respond to it in this particular way? Do I see my failures as information that will help me to get better? Or do my failed outcomes define me as a failure? Do I invest energy and succumb to emotional responses such as anger or frustration? Or do I choose not to get angry or frustrated and focus on the next task in the process of improvement? Answering questions such as these can help the athlete create new and effective strategies for managing failure and the inevitable adversity that comes with the pursuit of competitive excellence. I think it's much healthier and productive to be curious instead of furious.

We have discussed the importance of praise and coaches "catching athletes doing it right." More importantly, athletes must develop the ability to catch themselves doing it right as well. In terms of process, they have to focus on the skill, or part of a skill, that they are working on and celebrate the correct execution of that skill, regardless of the outcome. That will help them to reinforce the correct execution and increase the chances of repeating that motor pattern on the next opportunity to respond. Remember, mechanically efficient skill execution does not guarantee the desired outcome, it just increases the chances of that outcome happening more often.

I like to view outcomes through the lens of statistical probability. We have identified, through correlative analysis, the skills that are linked most highly to competitive success. We can also, through that same process, identify the skills that correlate most highly to losing. Most athletes only want to celebrate perfect outcomes. They tend to see sport as this zero-sum game, where it's either the acceptable level of "perfection" or something less, which is deemed to be unacceptable and therefore a failure. It's okay to be okay when you're learning, especially if your process is great, and we know that all that frustration is certainly not helping you get better. The self-talk and the praise-to-reprimand ratio get all messed up, as does the ability to learn or compete because we just won't have that many perfect outcomes to celebrate. We do, however, have many less-than-perfect outcomes that we can beat ourselves up over.

Instead of athletes only celebrating the best things that can happen, what if they could celebrate stopping the worst thing from happening? Isn't that worth celebrating too? In volleyball, perfect passes (serve receptions) help you win—but good passes do too. However, getting aced hurts the team's chances of winning more than passing perfectly helps them. So, even if you don't pass perfectly, the fact that you didn't get aced is a win and is therefore worth celebrating. I know this might seem like semantics, but I've seen this shift in perspective accelerate learning considerably.

Perspective is another critical part of the athlete's responsibility. People commonly have negativity bias, meaning that adverse events have a greater effect on a person's psychological state than positive ones. Even if the events are of the same magnitude, the positive one tends to have less of an impact on a person's thoughts and behavior. In other words, we feel negative things more intensely, and there is a tendency to amplify our shortcomings and make them more than they really are.[23] We are participating in sport, something that matters and that we care deeply about, but it's certainly not life or death.

As for losing, it happens and is, as I've said, an occupational hazard for anyone who competes, but we only lose if we waste the opportunity to learn. There are always wins to be had in sports and the pursuit of excellence. They might not always be on the scoreboard, but remember that you always have the power to define yourself. The score, the practice, the drill, or the particular repetition you're doing only has that power if you let it. As Viktor Frankl said in *Man's Search for Meaning*, "Everything can be taken from a person but one thing: the last of the human freedoms—to choose one's attitude in any given set of circumstances, to choose one's own way."[24]

We can be patient, urgent, and kind, but we can also approach the pursuit of excellence with grace and gratitude. There is immense power in living with an appreciative spirit.

COLUMN 2

	2
ATHLETE RESPONSIBILITIES	• Formulate skill schema
COACH RESPONSIBILITIES	• Develop motor program
GUIDING PRINCIPLES AND BEHAVIORS	• Specifity vs. generality • Transfer • Whole vs. part practice • State-dependent remembering • Blocked vs. random practice • Progressions

ATHLETE RESPONSIBILITIES

In practice, when you are learning skills, forming an accurate task schema, the mental representation of the required task is critical to its execution. As with any observational and visualization task, the more detail you can create in your schema, the better your chances of accurately recreating it.

COACH RESPONSIBILITIES

Once you've created your motor programs and skill constructs, you next have to figure out how to teach them. You need to understand the principles that guide motor program development and then determine the methods you should apply that will facilitate the most efficient and effective acquisition of the skills and systems we need to give ourselves the best chance of achieving the outcome goal.

GUIDING PRINCIPLES AND BEHAVIORS

Specificity vs. Generality

In a 1958 paper entitled "Specificity vs. Generality in Learning Motor Skills," F.M. Henry questioned the popular belief that motor abilities were, to a large extent, genetically determined.[25]

The idea of general athletic ability, that people are born with a fixed amount of universal athletic talent, is still a widely held opinion in sports. The idea of "the natural athlete" is compelling and convenient relative to our own athletic shortcomings, but there has never been a scientific study that supports its existence. The research does suggest that certain gene variants have been consistently associated with endurance or power-related performance, but these gene variants are not necessarily predictive of performance.[26]

A few years after Henry's work was first published, psychologist Edwin Fleischman (*Handbook of Human Abilities*) explored the concept of innate versus acquired abilities and motor skills in his book *The Structure and Measurement of Physical Fitness*.[27] He then continued to build on a body of work about the subject for decades. He suggested that we are born with a certain number of independent abilities that we draw on to complete mental, physical, or social tasks.

Fleischman eventually identified 73 separate human abilities (21 cognitive, 10 psycho-motor, 9 physical, 12 sensory/perception, 21 social/interpersonal). These are measurable and quantifiable abilities that we all have different amounts of. When we are presented with a task, we draw from a combination of these abilities to perform it. Different tasks require different abilities, and based on the amounts of those abilities we possess, the amount of practice and instruction we receive, and our motivation to perform the tasks, we are able to execute them at a certain level of competency. It's like having a tool kit. Different jobs require different tools, or even a different combination of tools. We all have the tools, but their quality, and our ability to use them, varies from person to person and task to task. Lastly, to be clear, abilities are not skills. Abilities are what we use to acquire and apply skills.

So what does all of that mean relative to the pursuit of excellence? The major implication pertains to how we train and practice. If tasks and skills are specific, we need to practice them in ways that are specific to that particular task. It also means that just because someone is great at soccer, that fact in no way means that they will be great or even good at golf. The fact that I can score 300 in bowling has no bearing on my ability to swim. Unitary athletic ability sounds good, but it just doesn't exist.

Softball pitcher Jennie Finch, an Olympic gold and silver medalist, lent very strong support to this fact by pitching to, and subsequently striking out three MLB hitters at the 2004 Pepsi All-Star Softball Game: Albert Pujols, the St. Louis Cardinals first baseman who would go on to be the National League MVP three times; New York Mets catcher Mike Piazza, a 12-time All-Star now in the Hall of Fame with 427 home runs; and Brian Giles, a two-time All-Star who ended up with a career batting average of .291, 287 home runs, and 1,078 RBIs. They could all hit baseballs coming from an overhand pitcher by attending to the relevant visual cues and then applying their hitting skill to contact the ball, but they couldn't pick up all of the cues from an underhand softball pitcher. They didn't know exactly what to look for, what to attend to, so they could not effectively apply their hitting skill.

Most people would agree that using a cylindrical bat to hit a ball that's moving quickly toward you would be a specific skill—and it is, but Jennie Finch demonstrated that it's actually much more specific than many would assume. It turns out that hitting a pitch from a softball pitcher requires hitting skills (where hitting would be visual and anticipatory skills in addition to the movements required to contact the ball) specific to softball.

Transfer

How much of what you do in practice transfers to what you hope to do in the moment of competition? If we are being efficient and effective with our coaching and teaching methods, then the rate of transfer should be high. Learning is difficult to quantify, but tracking performance is much easier. The easiest way to assess transfer would be to quantify changes in performance such as increases in speed, height of a jump, distances covered, points scored, and so on. These variables are much easier to assess than any measurable metric of learning.

When trying to describe the world of Olympic volleyball, I summarize it as four years of work with the hope to be good for two weeks, and then hope to be great for the last two hours. The weight of it all is very real, not just to medal but to even qualify, with 221 countries competing for only 11 spots at the Olympic Games.

My sense of urgency over the course of the quadrennials was real; I didn't think we had a second to spare. I also wanted to make sure that the things we did in practice had a high degree of transfer to what we had to do to win matches. If skills are specific, and we needed to get better at playing volleyball, then practice had to look a lot like playing volleyball.

For example, serving is a very important skill in our sport. Traditional serving practice constructs split the team into two groups, one at each end of the court, serving at each other for a set amount of time. The athletes get lots of repetitions, but those repetitions are not very game-like. In a volleyball match, serving occurs after a rally has ended, and then the server goes back to serve one serve, with no guarantee that there will be another. There's the referee's whistle, a target they need to hit, the crowd is going wild, and we're keeping score. As you can see, traditional practice repetitions do not closely represent serving in the game, and the amount of transfer is consequently low.

Is hitting a baseball off a tee the best way to improve the skill of hitting a pitched baseball? Do 50 mph pitches in the middle of the strike zone help you to get better at hitting 100 mph heat or an 80 mph sinker or curveball? Does blocking against inanimate football dummies or pushing weighted blocking sleds help football linemen become better at blocking a live opponent? I'm not sure. They might help, but they don't seem to resemble the game very much, and my guess is that the transfer between these practice activities and the moment of competition is fairly low.

Remember, it's not about right or wrong: the question is about effective and efficient methods. Do these practice activities transfer highly to what happens in the moment of competition? If they don't, we must ask ourselves, why are we doing them? Often, the answer is because we've always done them this way—it's tradition, and you know how I feel about that. It's important, and we absolutely should respect it, but it should never be the right reason for doing anything, unless it's the right reason.

Whole vs. Part Practice

If motor programs are specific and transfer is generally low between tasks, practicing the whole task should lead to learning that is more effective than practicing the parts of the task separately and then trying to put them all together.

Once you have created your skill constructs and identified your keys, you then have to decide how you are going to present them. This is not just a question of order, although your keys should be both incremental and sequential. The objective here is optimized learning. If I want to teach an athlete to spike a volleyball, I have to teach them how to approach, jump, get ready to hit, and make contact with the ball while in mid-air. What is the most effective and efficient way to teach all of that? Do I teach all of these elements at once? Do I just teach the approach for 15 minutes, then the jump for 15 minutes, then the arm swing, the contact, and try to add them all together at the end? The research says that the best way to teach skills is to do the whole skill while focusing solely on one part, or key, at a time. The benefit of this method is that the athlete learns, not only the part, but they also learn how the part fits into the whole. They acquire the part of the skill and the context for its application within the whole skill.

State-Dependent Remembering

State-dependent learning has been a well-known principle for quite a while. There are countless studies that verify home-court advantage. But it's the opportunity to create a game-like environment and game-like emotions that's equally, if not more, important. Big moments can evoke big emotional responses. Practicing big moments allows people the opportunity to learn how best to respond to those emotional responses. They can learn how to take a breath and get ready for the moment of competition.

We need to teach our athletes emotional control, the ability to be present and compete in the big moments. Creating these moments in practice gives them a chance to develop their ability to know what they have to do to win the next moment of competition, and be able to do it. The more we can make our practices look and feel like the sporting contest itself, the greater the amount of transfer we will have, and our athletes will also learn to get more comfortable being uncomfortable. They will learn to control themselves, giving them a chance to be in control of their performance.

Blocked vs. Random Practice

Every practice should be planned, but many coaches also believe that practice should be an exercise in precision and control. They want it to be algorithmic, controlled inputs leading to controlled outputs and consistent outcomes. Practices that are highly structured and highly controlled look good, but the reality of sport (and life) is that it can be quite messy, and that's okay. As much as you want to believe that standing in the "right" spot means the ball will come to you, that isn't what often happens. Learning to make sense of the chaos is critical to success.

Controlling practice is similar to learning how to ride a bike using training wheels. You learn to pedal and steer, but you miss out on the most critical element of bike-riding success: balance.

When you compete, anything can happen, and that randomness should be embraced and practiced. The more variables we control, the fewer opportunities we give our athletes to learn. This is a tough challenge for many coaches because it's so much easier to monitor progress in skill acquisition in a controlled environment than skill application in the context of randomness. In the former case, it's a binary challenge: the athlete either did or didn't do it. The athlete was in the right position to make the play, or they weren't. The ball hit the target, or it didn't. In the realm of skill application, however, the considerations are far more nuanced: we have to help our athletes make the right choice at the time. If the athlete was in the right position, why and how did they decide to get there? If they attempted to make the play, why did they make the choice that they made?

When you teach to something as critical and somewhat nebulous as reading the game, and reading the game is a huge differentiating factor between the "greats" and the "goods" in any sport, you shift into the role of Socratic teacher, engaging in a cooperative dialogue with your athletes. You stimulate critical thinking, which becomes part of the process of skill application. It's an important coaching tool relative to developing decision-making.

The popular narrative regarding notable athletes is that they are so physically superior that their talent alone is the differentiating factor for their greatness. Anyone who has been at an elite level in a sport can tell you that this is seldom the case. Sure, there are some people who are freakishly good athletically, and those physical talents and abilities can predispose someone to a high level of success in the sport. However, there are also some people that are freakishly physically talented in their sport but are not dominant.

If we use the ecological concept of food chains as an analogy for the level of competition in sports, as you go further up the food chain, the physical elements you bring are not going to be as much of a differentiating factor as they may have been at lower levels. For example, being faster or stronger may have been a differentiator on your high-school team, but at the top of the food chain everyone is an apex predator, everyone is fast and strong. The differentiating factors therefore become fundamental mastery of skills, repeatability, mental resilience, making the right choice at the right time, and being a great teammate.

Physical talent and skill application come together for the superior performer; the two form a point of connection that is not taught to enough, mainly because it's difficult to teach. Teaching an athlete to perform a skill is a more clearly defined process than the idea of helping the athlete interpret the competitive environment and select the appropriate response. However, when they learn this skill, the randomness of a competitive situation becomes less random, because the athlete now has an enhanced ability to evaluate a situation and distill the number of possibilities for "what happens next" from an extremely large number of potential outcomes to only one or two. Those who can read the game, see the play evolve, understand what they are seeing, and can anticipate or predict the next play with a high degree of accuracy possess a significant competitive advantage. They are free to compete with composure and control. Those who can't, compete in a constant state of reaction and surprise.

Learning to read the situation supports and augments the athlete's competitive intention. The opportunity to play to "what is" makes a quantifiable difference in performance and outcome. Blocked practice environments do not help an athlete cultivate the competitive advantage that reading presents. Random practice environments that are game-like or sport-like do. You need to train to reality, and the reality of sports is that anything can happen.

Progressions
Progressions represent the sequence or order you use to present your keys. The order that you think will best facilitate the athlete's learning of the skill. Your keys are the chunked pieces of information you have created to describe the critical elements

of the skill; the progressions are the order in which you present and teach those keys. Your progressions should be incremental and sequential.

For example, when learning to spike a volleyball, you should start with your footwork. Once that is in place, you can work on your double arm lift and jump, then you get ready to hit (load), and finally you hit the ball (unload). However, if you do not get your footwork right, then your arm lift will be inefficient, which will end up compromising your load and unload.

Here is how keys and progressions work together to teach spiking in volleyball:

1. Footwork—number of steps, size, speed, position, and distance from the net.
2. Double arm-lift—arms swing down, forward, backward, up. Long and loose to jump high and load fast.
3. Load—hitting arm up and back, non-hitting arm up and pointing at the ball.
4. Unload—stay tall, non-hitting arm down, torque to generate arm speed, contact high and in front.

You could teach the same thing in 20 progressions, but by chunking information (saying a little but meaning a lot), we can simplify the process and reduce the mental load. Aim for as few keys as possible and communicate them to the athlete in an efficient and effective way, while making sure your progressions match the sequencing of the skill.

COLUMN 3

	3
ATHLETE RESPONSIBILITIES	• Attempt skill
COACH RESPONSIBILITIES	• Optimize responses
GUIDING PRINCIPLES AND BEHAVIORS	• Practice environment • Practice • Opportunities to respond • Massed vs. distributed practice • Drill constructs • Fatigue • Mental engagement

ATHLETE RESPONSIBILITIES

We talked earlier about the difference between sweating and practicing. I currently coach at a university, and I tell our athletes that volleyball will probably be the hardest class that they take here, for a couple of reasons. First, because people's expectation of practice is generally more about sweating than learning. Second, there's a lot to learn. There are a lot of skills, systems, and other physical, mental, and social skills they have to acquire.

When you attempt the skill, try and do it with the desired change in place. That requires a physical and mental commitment to making the change. Most athletes aren't used to that degree of task focus or the uncomfortable feelings that can come with it. The main barrier in this process is the outcome. Athletes will forgo the required change in pursuit of the "right" outcome, because that's how they have previously received their praise and reinforcement, and consequently their identity and self-worth might be more connected to their outcomes. As we've said, not everyone is comfortable getting a little bit worse to get a whole lot better, so we have to find value and reason for celebration in the process. You need to learn to catch yourself doing it right. Celebrate the parts of the skill you are doing well—it leads to better learning and retention. Let your coach identify and speak to the inefficiencies.

COACH RESPONSIBILITIES

The coach's job is to create an environment that optimizes their athletes' responses. Make sure the physical practice environment is safe, that you've created the best skill constructs and keys that you can, that you've planned your practice and that you have skill learning and skill application in the practice plan with drill constructs that can facilitate the acquisition of both.

We talked earlier about our athletes having to "cross the line," and the coach needs to do that as well. Regardless of whatever concerns or issues your day presented, you have to be able to compartmentalize those and focus on the task at hand, which is running the best practice you can. If you bring your personal issues to the practice environment, you will reduce learning. The coach sets the temperature in the room, so if the athletes have to worry about whether you'll be happy, or sad, or angry, or sullen, or giddy, you'll compromise your ability to develop trust with your athletes. They won't feel safe, and practices will not be as efficient and effective as they could be. What you have to do is cross the line and be a consistent source of relevant knowledge and information that shows genuine care and concern for those you coach. Your stuff is your stuff; practice is about them.

Lastly, I said that coaches set the temperature in the room, but they also need to read the room. If the drill isn't going well, or an athlete is struggling, or everyone seems tired, it's up to you to find ways to reconnect your athletes to the practice content. Change the drill, the skill, or the emphasis to try to shift the energy. You also should consider stopping early if the work is getting done or if, try as you may, you can't salvage a bad practice. You can reward great practices by stopping at a point when the effort or level of execution is high, but you shouldn't flog a dead horse. If the practice isn't going well, cut your losses and try again next time.

GUIDING PRINCIPLES AND BEHAVIORS

Practice Environment

The practice environment is the space in which you train. For practice to be as efficient and effective as possible, we need it to be safe, in a lot of different ways. First, and perhaps most obvious, is making the training space as safe as we can from causing the athletes any physical harm. Making sure the equipment is in good condition, that the playing surface is good, that any sharp edges are covered or padded, and so on.

The environment also needs to be safe for the athletes to learn, where *safe* means there is trust and all of the mental and emotional safety that is required for the learning process to occur. Learning will be compromised if the coach and/or the athletes make the environment unsafe by punishment, judgment, or any other such negative consequence. The athlete may disengage and not be vulnerable enough to make the changes they need to make.

I think there is also merit in keeping people not associated with your athlete or team out of the practice environment, so that the athletes aren't distracted and can feel comfortable enough to make mistakes and learn from them. I don't think you have to have closed practices, but if there are people there, they need to be people you know and trust.

Practice

I have said that practice is the battle you must win. What I mean by that is that you must try to get everything you can out of your practices. Make as much improvement as possible and don't waste a second, because what you're battling every day is time and complacency. We do not have an unlimited amount of time to get these skills and systems in place: our goal is time-bound, so we have to try to get the most out of every moment that we're practicing. As for complacency, the temptation to take your foot off the gas is real. Can I go a little easier today? You could, but you would not be honoring your commitment to competitive excellence. As we have said, the margins in competition, especially at the higher levels, are extremely thin, and championships will be won and lost by a point or two, a play here, a decision there. Olympic medals are won or lost by hundredths of seconds and fractions of points. Winning the practice battle means your athletes consistently train with the intent, work-rate, and discipline required. It's not punitive, and it doesn't mean they can't have fun, but if we know the margins are thin, then every play, every day matters. Each repetition is a chance to get closer to the goal.

To start, you should base your practice activities on the outcome goal, the task goals (required skills and level of execution), and from there, try to establish your daily goal for that practice. You should also consider the practice parameters and resources that you have. The biggest constraint we have is time. How long is your competitive season? How many competitions do you have each week? How many practices can you hold each week? How many hours do your get for each day of practice? Once we know our time, we can make better decisions regarding its use.

There are other constraints to consider as well. The physical resources at your disposal matter. The number of courts, or hoops, lanes, or fields. The number of balls, boats, racquets, or pucks. Your roster size can influence drill structure, and the number of coaches can also influence how you run your drills and your feedback frequency. If you can plan a practice that takes all of this into consideration and maximizes your athletes' opportunities to respond, their opportunities for feedback, and transfer, then that's a win. And the reason you must get the win in practice is because, in large part, you control it.

Planning effective and efficient practices is a critical part of competitive excellence. And to be clear, by *plan*, I mean you need to take the time to plan them and write them down. Don't just show up with an idea in your head and wing it, take the time to plan it. What are we going to do today? What skills? What drills? Are we learning? Are we competing? What goal and/or intention are we committing to that will get us another step closer to our outcome goal?

Some coaches like to create long-range practice plans outlining their intended path to the outcome goal, but I don't think you want to get too far ahead of yourself. Have an outline for the skills and systems you want to work on and the type of practice drills or activities you want to do over the course of a week. I think that's far enough out. The weekly plan is based on our task goals and where the athletes are relative to their acquisition and application. Planning practice activities a month, a season, or a year in advance might not be the most efficient use of your time. You should map out your daily practice outlines for the week using a basic practice grid, with your practice days as the columns, and the skills, systems, activities, and drills you want to work on each day as the rows.

Start the week with the most important skills you need to work on. If you make the desired progress in one day, move on to the next day's practice outline and the next skill. If you don't, I recommend you spend more time on that skill the next day— until you've made the progress you want to make. Moving on to a different skill just because it's written in your weekly practice grid makes no sense.

In terms of executing the daily practice plan, there is an overall structure that I like. Start by writing practice where it can be seen. A whiteboard, a smartboard, a screen, somewhere the athletes can see the skills, systems, drills, and activities you've planned to work on. This allows them to connect their goals to your practice plan and will alleviate any questions or concerns regarding what practice activities they'll be doing that day. It provides clarity, facilitates focus, and shows your athletes that you're not just making it up as you go along.

If athletes want to come to practice early and get some one-on-one coaching, or even one-on-two or -three, then they should. Individual or small group pre-practice work can be very beneficial. A short amount of time each day with focused instruction can accelerate learning significantly. As an aside, you can do post-practice individual or small group work as well!

I also really like some time for "vitamins," that is, your athlete's daily dose of fundamentals (a term and concept created by the NBA's San Antonio Spurs). Athletes work for five to 10 minutes with a coach in small groups and focus on fundamental skill elements specific to their position or to that sport.

Warming up is important, but the purpose of practice is to change performance—to improve it. We want to use the time we have as efficiently and effectively as possible, so when designing practices and drills, we have a lot of decisions to make about what activities we're going to do relative to our time constraints. If an athlete is going to warm up by running for five minutes instead of warming up with dynamic activities related to the sport, then we've lost an opportunity to work on those relevant motor patterns. For example, a volleyball player could do spike approach footwork, or blocking footwork, or transition footwork as a submaximal warm-up activity that is also reinforcing motor patterns that are relevant to volleyball. The time and number of repetitions the athletes gain by warming up this way quickly add up over the course of a season, and our practices become more efficient and effective. Running might get you warm, but it only makes you better at running.

To start practice, you should talk with the athletes about the objectives for the day, and usually you would do this where the practice plan is displayed. While you might connect the day's activities to the outcome goal, you certainly want to connect the practice to your task goals and daily goals, and then get to work on learning and/or competing. If you want to teach in your practice, start teaching right out of the gate. As the physical demands and fatigue increase, the capacity for learning will decrease, so learn while the athletes are fresh. Work on your big-rock skills in a controlled environment and then build into a more game-like environment in which those skills are applied. Small group activities, playing the sport in smaller groups—often in smaller spaces—allows for a game-like environment but also increases the athlete's opportunities to respond.

To finish practice, I like to play something that looks a lot like the sport or the moment of competition itself. In these types of drill constructs, you can add goals for the drill or have different areas of skill or system emphasis. The last thing to consider is physical conditioning in practice. We have to be conscious of time, so devise drills where you can increase the intensity and get an anaerobic/aerobic training effect while still doing something that looks like your sport. Sprints get you better at sprinting and, yes, there is a physiological effect, but you can generate a similar physiological response and get better at your sport by using a high intensity drill for physical conditioning.

Opportunities to Respond

One of the main goals of your practice design is to maximize the number of opportunities to respond. The more opportunities to respond, the more opportunities for learning and feedback, and the faster the rate of improvement.

In youth sports in particular, maximizing the number of repetitions that each athlete has during practice is critical to improvement. Generally speaking, youth teams practice only two or three times a week, for an hour or two at a time, so making sure you get the highest number of quality repetitions in each practice session should be the goal. If you're lining up 12 kids at the free throw line, each taking a turn to shoot at one basket, while there are three other hoops available in the gym, you are doing your athletes a significant disservice. If each shot takes 20 seconds, 12 kids at one hoop each get one shot every four minutes. Three kids at four hoops gives each kid a shot every minute and the opportunity for better engagement, more feedback, and better learning.

Massed vs. Distributed Practice

Research on massed practice suggests that doing something repeatedly, for long periods of time and without a break, does not make you significantly better by the end of the session. It makes you bored. You may see some improvement at first, but then you'll see a low or even diminishing return on that investment of practice time. Distributing the repetitions over the course of the practice session is more effective. Working on a skill for four different sessions of 15 minutes interspersed throughout a practice will lead to more effective learning than one continuous session of 60 minutes.

Drill Constructs

We have said that we want our drills to be game-like to maximize transfer but we can't always do drills that exactly replicate the game or moment of competition. This doesn't mean that we can't have transfer occur, we just have to design our drills to be as game-like as possible. When trying to devise these constructs, you should consider elements of your sport such as the athlete's location in the field of play, how they move in that space, the sequence and timing of the skills or events in your sport, how the drill is initiated, and how the drill ends. You should design drills that maximize opportunities to respond and opportunities for feedback and transfer.

Some coaches like to have a drill for everything. We don't have many drills that we use because we need them to adhere to our guiding principles. If we want practice activities to be game-like, there are only so many ways a drill can be like the game. What we do have, though, are many different ways we can modify the drills to train the skills or systems that we want to improve.

When I think about the seemingly endless quest for drills, I'm reminded of this quote from author George Leonard in his book *Mastery*: "The essence of boredom is to be found in the obsessive search for novelty. Satisfaction lies in mindful repetition, the discovery of endless richness in subtle variations on familiar themes."[28] You do not need 300 drills. A few drills that can be modified a lot of different ways will do. We want our athletes to invest their mental energy in learning new skills and systems, not in an endless variety of new drills.

Some of these drill variations or modifications include things such as time constraints, that is, doing a certain skill for a set period of time. In-a-row scores—having to repeat a certain skill and/or repeat that skill at a certain level of execution for a predetermined number of repetitions is another possibility. If the athlete makes a mistake, they can go back to zero and start over. Or, you can have constructs where they have x number of opportunities to get the in-a-row goal. Similarly, we could use x out of y scoring, you have to get x number of repetitions at a required level of execution in y attempts. Scoring systems can also be modified. Adding extra repetitions in a game-like environment creates more opportunities to respond and is a great way to increase the intensity of the drill (think physical conditioning). Awarding bonus points for skills or outcomes that we want to direct the athlete's attentional focus to, is also effective. They allow you to emphasize or focus on the desired skill without having to make significant changes to the drill construct.

You can also adjust the constraints of a drill. For example, this sequence has to include this specific play, or maybe one of these two options. You can start the drill a certain way or demand that the drill can only finish a certain way. If you keep score in your sport, you can start the drill at a certain score. If your sport is played for time, you can start the drill with two minutes to go. You can also adjust the physical constraints of the drill by doing things such as adjusting the size of the field of play (make the space smaller or bigger) or by creating targets.

In team sports, one of the considerations is who plays with or against whom in practice? Do the starters always play together? Is it always A-squad versus B-squad? Or should you mix and match your practice lineups? I have found, at every level that I've coached, that mixing the lineups makes for better practices. Your starting lineup should be one of the lineups in the mix, but the parity created by balancing your practice teams leads to a better level of competition, which then leads to better engagement and learning. Having everyone play with and against everyone benefits everyone. It also helps you when you compete. For example, if a player is injured, we can make substitutions and not worry about the effectiveness of different lineups, because the athletes have all already played together in practice.

Before practice starts, the coaches should meet and review the day's activities to suggest any changes and to make sure everyone is clear on their coaching responsibilities in each drill. As practice unfolds, you should be conscious of the flow, the feel of it. If it's getting bogged down, you should intervene and possibly change the drill to try and change the energy. The flow of practice matters—having everyone engaged and on-task makes for better learning. Another consideration is when to stop practice. If we've worked hard, done great work, and we're getting fatigued, I'm fine finishing practice early. However, if I only have a couple of days a week to train, I would be more inclined to use all of the practice time I'm given. But, like all of this, you get to decide.

Fatigue

The effect of fatigue on learning is real. When you're tired, you don't learn as well as when you're rested. So, if you want to teach a new skill or system, teach it at the beginning of your practice. One former athlete told me her gymnastics coach used to have everyone run around a football field three times before going into the gym for practice. That kind of warm-up violates the law of specificity (running makes you better at running, not gymnastics), but it can also fatigue the learner to the point where new skill development is impeded. I cannot imagine running half a mile and then trying to learn a back handspring.

Fatigue can also hinder performance. Shooting free throws at the end of a physically demanding basketball game is different from shooting them while the athlete is fresh and rested. So we not only have to consider the role of fatigue in learning, we also have to learn to manage it as a possible factor in competition.

There are two considerations here: one is that we should look to train our free throws a couple of different ways. If we're learning and working on improving our free throw skill, we should do that at the beginning of practice. If we're training to skill application and specificity, though, we should sometimes practice shooting free throws at the end of practice, when the athletes are more fatigued. This is a practice condition that better represents the game, and it's therefore more likely to facilitate transfer.

The second consideration is that we need to physically condition our athletes. We need to train their strength, quickness, endurance, and cardiovascular systems. None of this is punitive; we are not training just to train. Athletes need to build their engines so they can resist the mental and physical degradation from fatigue and can recover more quickly during, and in-between, contests or practices.

Lastly, mental fatigue is a real phenomenon as well, especially when we are asking our athletes to engage in deliberate practice activities that are predicated on intense and unsustainable mental focus. Brains are similar to muscles in that they can develop and adapt—neuroplasticity is real. However, like muscles, brains also need time to recover.

Mental Engagement

The body can't do anything without the mind telling it what to do. That is a fact. And yet we tend to train the body and the mind as separate systems, when it's clear that they are inextricably connected. I am not a sports psychologist, but I know about the mental game. I incorporate what I believe are the simplest and most effective mental skills into our program. They are breathing, routines, self-talk, visualization, body language, emotional control, and journaling.

Learning to take a breath—all of the way in and all of the way out, finishing it—is an important skill. Oxygenating the lungs oxygenates the brain, and that is vital to thinking and decision-making. The breath can also give us pause and can facilitate some clarity in moments of chaos. It affords us a space between our emotional responses and our subsequent actions.

Once your skill level is sufficient, you should develop performance routines. Routines are extremely helpful in closed-loop activities (a task where you are in control of all the elements of the skill, such as shooting a free throw or hitting a golf ball). They can also help you prepare and refocus before executing in open-loop activities as well (where there are more random variables in the system—that is, other people or a ball). Routines can add an important layer of consistency to skill execution in either environment.

Self-talk is a huge part of the mental game, and it plays a significant role in the athlete's path to competitive excellence. Learning to control your inner narrative is critical. Every cell in your body is listening to your thoughts, so the things you say to yourself matter. The narrative in the athlete's head is the most important voice in this process.

Negative self-talk usually occurs when we have an emotional response to an outcome. That emotional self-talk produces more emotional responses and the subsequent chemicals that get released into the body. There is a mental and physiological effect to emotion. Athletes tend to be very hard on themselves. Again, their base expectation is often perfection, and the self-talk is often framed and phrased in absolutes—*I have to*, *I must*, *I need to*. But softening that language can alter the emotional effect, before and after the behavior is executed—*I'd like to*, *I hope to*, *I want to*. These phrases still covey the appropriate intention, but the emotional stakes associated with the outcome are different, and the mental and physiological responses are too.

As we've learned, negativity bias is real and the language we tend to use in our self-talk reflects that. "This is terrible," and, "I can't take this anymore," might be phrases we use, but they are unlikely to be based in reality. We are playing sports, and we are already more fortunate than most—your current circumstance might be uncomfortable, but it's probably not terrible. You can't take it anymore? Well, you probably can actually. After all, we are just playing a game. It's not starvation or a terminal illness. By using language that amplifies the negativity, even if that language is "normalized" and part of the current lexicon, you produce emotional responses and all of the mental and physical consequences that go with them. There is a cumulative negative effect.

Negative bias is also manifested in another way through our self-talk—the self put-down. We are generally not very nice to ourselves. We say things that we would never say to others, and yet somehow we think that it's okay or acceptable to say them to ourselves. "I'm a loser," "I suck," "This always happens to me." It's not forgive and forget, it's forgive and learn. It is tough enough making changes or competing against an opponent; you should not be an additional barrier to your own learning and achievement.

Connected to self-talk is visualization. Can you see yourself making the required changes and succeeding? There is scientific evidence supporting the idea that visualization can affect change, that observational learning or reminiscence can result in a gain in learning or performance without practice. You can get better at physical skills just by envisioning them. But you have to think about them the right way, the depth of sensory feeling and your ability to control your images matters. In fact, you could say that "seeing it" is just the beginning. You can also learn to feel and even hear your performance outcomes. This additional layering of sensory perception is called "sensualization," the value and mechanics of which are described by leading extreme athletes in the book *Lessons from the Edge.*[29] Sensualization can afford even greater possibilities for change.

Many people struggle with imagery because they try it and are not very good at it; they get despondent, and the subsequent self-talk is generally not very good either. Then, because people tend to not enjoy things that they are not good at, they give up. Stick with it, practice visualizing regularly, start small and simple and build the capacity to visualize from there. It will help you learn and change more quickly.

We also need to consider our body language. Our non-verbal communication is powerful. Often times we are saying a lot without speaking a word. Studies have addressed what the percentage break-down of our communication is between verbal and non-verbal, but experts generally concur that somewhere between 70 and 93 percent of our communication is nonverbal. Albert Mehrabian's research in the 1960s is particularly pertinent to sports because he focused on the communication of emotion. In his study, subjects had to rate the feelings of a speaker after listening to different words. The words spoken and tone of voice sometimes didn't match, and it was the tone of voice that won out in terms of what the listeners heard. Saying, "I'm happy," in an angry tone did not convince the listener that the subject was happy. A similar outcome was observed when the verbally expressed emotion was connected to a disparate body movement. You can say, "I'm sorry!" to someone, but if your fist is clenched and you are scowling while you're saying it, your apology will probably not be accepted. Our actions do speak louder than our words, and how we say something matters more than what we say, and what we don't say matters the most!

Many people have seen Amy Cuddy's TED talk on power poses. Our body position influences how we actually feel. Standing tall, raising your arms in a V, and smiling all have positive physical and mental benefits. Body language also sends messages to your teammates and opponents as well. It can communicate that you are present and ready to compete, or that you're defeated and ready to give up. Your sphere of influence is bigger than you know, and your body language is saying a lot without you speaking a word.

The stress or anxiety connected to the moment of competition is real and presents itself in many different ways. Most commonly, we think about anxiety, choking or a reduction in performance level caused by the pressure or expectation of the moment. While choking can certainly be an issue, there are other powerful stressors and emotions that learning and competition can evoke. Responses such as fear of failure, anxiety over the expectations of self and others, anger over a bad call, the desire for adulation and validation, or even arrogance over having handed your opponent a soul-crushing blow can all take vital energy and focus away from the task at hand.

How you respond to emotion, especially negative emotion, matters. I like to talk to our athletes about creating consistent energy as opposed to being on the roller coaster of emotion. I do that because I want our athletes to stay in a rational space of control and intention as opposed to the more irrational space of emotion. However, I know that we won't, and we shouldn't, try to eradicate or replace emotion with energy. What we must do is teach our athletes how to control emotion and channel it.

Emotional control is not emotional repression. We tend to teach our boys to hide their emotions, to bury them in some stoic display of manhood. We also tend to accept that our girls are emotional as a circumstance of their gender and physiology. Boys don't cry, but girls do. It all speaks to the not so thinly veiled misogynistic narrative of weakness. We will address this concept of emotional control in more detail later in the book, but just understand that it plays a significant role in the process of competitive excellence.

Another important mental mechanism for facilitating learning is journaling. Journaling is simply writing down your thoughts and feelings to understand them more clearly. A safe place to confess your struggles and fears without judgment or punishment. It can feel good to get all of your thoughts and feelings out of your head, where they can float around endlessly and consume valuable time and energy, and put them down or paper or type them on a device. This not only helps to declutter the mind; it affords reflection, introspection, and perspective, as well as change and intention. In the sporting context, write about questions or intentions—for example, *How am I doing relative to my performance goals? Was the mistake I made today as big of a deal as I made it out to be? Next time I will try to respond in this way,* or, *Next practice I am going to build on the last one by holding on to the changes I made and working on this next part of the skill I'm trying to improve.* I addition to clarity, journaling can help with stress, anxiety, and especially with emotional control.

Another important journaling tool is writing down why you enjoy playing or doing your sport. What makes it fun and enjoyable? The reason for this is because inevitably, at some point, your sport will become challenging and difficult, and it won't be as much fun. In those tough times, having a reminder of why you're there, why you are doing this, why you love to play or compete will hold you in good stead.

Journaling works for some athletes, and for others it's not that effective. Try it for a while and see where it takes you. Ultimately, it should be something you want to do, instead of something you have to do. However, the most important thing is the act of reflection—that has to happen.

There is another "mental" skill that we must teach as well, and that is fundamental skill mastery. This is a critical, and often overlooked, component of the mental game. Your mental skills won't help very much if your physical skills aren't up to par. You might have the greatest pre–free throw routine in the world, but if the mechanics of your shooting action are off, then the routine won't matter. You can bounce the ball three times and say your mantra, but it'll still be a brick, not because your mental game is deficient but because you're just not very good. So many people see deficiencies in performance as a mental shortcoming, when more often than not it's a physical or technical one. Technical mastery is a cornerstone of the mental game, and skill confidence is 100 percent connected to skill competence.

All these mental skills can help your athlete to learn in practice and do their job in competition. It is easy to be good when it's easy to be good, but I believe that true championship behavior is defined by how you manage the tough times. What do you do when it's difficult, overwhelming, and hard? You're exhausted, but the job's not done. You make the play, but the referee makes a bad call against you. How do you respond? Are you angry? Frustrated? Defeated? Do you suddenly play not to lose instead of playing to win? Or do you take a deep breath and get on with the task at hand?

Dr. Ken Ravizza had many great quotes about performing under duress. There are a couple that I find particularly pertinent to learning and competition. The first is this: "Are you that bad that you have to feel good to play good?" It's a great question! Can we only perform when the conditions are optimal? Given how often conditions are optimal (spoiler alert: it's not often), separating how we feel about the moment of competition and focusing instead on what you have to do to succeed in that moment is critical. Whatever you feel about the moment, the moment doesn't feel anything about you! As Ravizza would say (the second great quote), "Can you have a good crummy day?" Can you give the team 100 percent of the 60 percent you have right now? The good news is you can. By learning to control yourself, you can learn to control your performance.

Interview with Sarah Wilhite

Sarah Wilhite currently plays professional volleyball in Japan. She was an alternate for Team USA's indoor women's volleyball team at the 2020 Olympic Games and has been on the national team since graduating from the University of Minnesota in 2016. Sarah played in different capacities all four years of her collegiate career, but never received any awards or accolades for her play until her senior year. In Sarah's last year of collegiate competition, she was named National Player of the Year by the AVCA and ESPNW, was the Big Ten Conference Player of the Year, and was recognized as a first-team All-American.

Let's talk about blending the mental game into the physical part of competition. When you joined the team as a freshman, you obviously had physical talents and abilities, but I think it was safe to say that your ability to perform at a high level was inconsistent. How did you feel about that?

Sarah Wilhite: I remember a preseason tournament or a preseason game where I performed really well, and I felt great. And then we started playing against stronger competition, and I was all of a sudden doubting all of the skills that I thought I had. I didn't have a lot of patience with myself. I remember being in matches, and if I messed up on the first attack of the game, or sometimes even in warmups, I was kind of out of it for the rest of the game. I just had this really unrealistic pressure that I put on myself to be perfect—even though I was nowhere near perfect fundamentally.

Did you recognize that there was a space in terms of your perception of your ability to execute the fundamental skills of the game and your actual ability?

SW: I knew I had these inefficiencies in my game. In high school, I was never really pushed mentally or technically. But it didn't really matter. I could get away with those inefficiencies at that level. And so, freshman year of college, there was a space where I thought, *Oh, man, I actually have a lot to work to do!* That was uncomfortable for me. It was hard for me to play with that uncomfortable feeling.

Did that awareness lead to the doubts, like, "Maybe I'm not as good as I think I am?" How did the pressure manifest itself?

SW: I was worried about the result, which is the worst thing you can do. You're trying to get better at a skill, and naturally, you get worse before you get better. When I was in that space of realizing I had a lot of things to figure out and I was not performing the way I wanted, it was uncomfortable. My results weren't there because it's a process. I would say that discomfort was definitely a piece of why I couldn't perform at my best or didn't have the confidence to perform at my best.

And there were times, Sarah, where you could see it was overwhelming. You could feel it. And we had to talk about it—that feeling that you couldn't get the job done.

SW: It was a mental block. Like in practice, when I was working on my approach and I'd do it well once and say, "Oh, yay. Things are clicking!" But then the next three I'd do it wrong and get frustrated. And I remember you would always say, and still do, "Don't get angry, get better." But I was there getting angry way before I was getting better.

And do you think that mental block was connected to self-talk like, "This sucks," "I suck"? Or was it more like, "I'm overwhelmed," more like cognitive overload?

SW: I think a combination of both. I for sure told myself, "I can't do this. I can't do this." I'd repeat that over and over again until my body started believing me, and I really couldn't do it.

Self-Fulfilling...

SW: I would just think, *I'll never get there. I'll never be able to make all of these small changes to make the bigger changes.*

Let's talk about sophomore year. How did it change after you got one year under your belt?

SW: That was 2014, and we weren't very good. We had all the stuff going on with changing the culture that year. A lot happened that spring, but the good stuff was discovering the ability to work hard as a team. On the mental side, I still had some struggles, but I remember that spring, we were just getting our butts kicked over and over again. And I think that brought our team together. Work hard and work through it together—that's what it was about.

It all goes hand in hand: the weight room, the recovery, all that stuff with learning on the court. Learning how to push through being uncomfortable in a workout helps you be able to push through being uncomfortable on the court.

So then you were going into your junior year, and I remember there were a few times we talked about the mental side of things. Tell me about that—those meetings and how that process was.

SW: I think a lot of those meetings I would get emotional, and I still had some blocks up about who I wanted to be and how I wanted to get there. Those meetings weren't really about volleyball, we'd focus mostly on the mental game and emotional control. We talked about managing expectations—mine and the expectations coming from others, social media even—managing the pressure of it all.

I think I put this unrealistic pressure on myself. We talked a lot about self-talk, too. I feel like I was my harshest critic, and that's when you would remind me that feedback on my performance isn't personal. It's about learning and taking another step forward. At some point, I got it.

I remember in a game, I think it was later in my senior year, but it was a moment I still remember. We were playing the No. 1 team in the country at the time—we were ranked second—so a huge game. We lost the first two sets. In any other year I would have thought, *We're screwed. I can't do this.* But then I said to myself, *I can do this. We can do this. I trust what we've put in.* It was just a moment I can look back on that was so freeing. I would have never thought that before. I remember you saying after the second set, "Hey, we're giving these guys way too much credit right now. We've just got to get back to doing what we do."

I remember saying, *Oh, you're right. I believe you!* deep in my body. *Yeah. I believe. Yeah. Yeah. We can do this. I can do this.* Trust it and go, and, sure enough, we won. It was a big deal.

You started to figure things out by your junior year, we had a great season in 2015. You had that next summer, and then you came into your senior year, and things were significantly different. What can you tell me about that?

SW: We had great players on our team, lots of All-Americans that junior year—and when Daly left there was a big space to step into. I think that opportunity helped push me to make changes in my mental game. We had a great culture, too, as a team. I feel like every single practice that we walked into, we all wanted to get better. You and the other coaches helped us create that. Just knowing my role and knowing the load that I would be carrying, I had this shift of being excited about that, versus seeing it as pressure, like, "I want to do this instead of I have to do this."

Would you say that sense of opportunity helped you to overcome the fear?

SW: It definitely helped. It was almost like I didn't have a choice but to see the opportunity.

You were certainly ready for it. You know what I mean? If it had presented itself to you as a freshman, I'm not sure you would have embraced it as wholeheartedly as you did as a senior.

SW: Yeah. I think those obstacles and roadblocks [I] kind of pushed through my first three years led me to be able to take advantage of that opportunity. If it had come earlier, maybe I would have reverted to that high school mentality, just wanting to be comfortable, you know, and not doing the hard work.

In the conference, you knew it was going to be a battle every night, and every weakness was going to be exposed. So you not only had to manage your skills, you also had to manage failure and adversity.

But it was so powerful doing something alongside people with the same intention. That is my sweet spot—I just feel really good when I'm the most connected to the people around me. Everyone wants what's best for the person next to them. And that just brings out the best in you.

I remember one game where I wasn't playing well. [A teammate] came up to me and said, "I know you know that you're not playing your A game right now, but we just need you to act like you're playing your A game for this team." It made a difference. It was a nice way of saying, "Get your head out of your you-know-what and be there for your team." Put the mental game into gear.

How have the lessons that helped you develop your mental game affected the rest of your life?

SW: Being in a foreign country and playing professionally involves a great deal of change. It's not comfortable. Everything seems different. You don't understand anything in a grocery store, and you can barely communicate with some of your teammates and things like that. But that idea of being comfortable being uncomfortable was something that I learned at Minnesota, and it has helped. And also, what I was saying before about my sweet spot, when I'm playing my best is when I'm the most connected, that still carries on to playing professionally. I know the importance of being a good teammate and getting to know people. Even though there are people on the team who don't speak English, we can still be connected in other ways.

COLUMN 4

	4
ATHLETE RESPONSIBILITIES	• Process feedback
COACH RESPONSIBILITIES	• Give initial and augmented feedback
GUIDING PRINCIPLES AND BEHAVIORS	• Feedback • Teach to the relevant key • Goals for drills • Competition • Testing • Data

ATHLETE RESPONSIBILITIES

Feedback is information, nothing more. The grass is green; the sky is blue; this is what you did on that last skill attempt. Do your best to not personalize or internalize the information. You're still a good person, and we like you very much, but you have this technical inefficiency that we'd like you to change. Take the information and do your best to apply it in practice, and then in competition.

COACH RESPONSIBILITIES

We have talked about communication, and when you're giving feedback, you have to be mindful of your delivery. You are giving specific information, so the content matters. I suggest you use or, at the very least, refer to your keys when giving feedback. It's efficient—the chunks of information say a little but mean a lot—and the keys become part of your cultural language, which gives them more power.

Being mindful of Mehrabian's research on communication might help you modulate your tone and be deliberate in your body language as well. Feedback offered in a steady measured tone is likely to be better received than feedback that's yelled. A calm neutral body position projects a neutral demeanor.

I suggest you stay clear of sarcasm in your coaching—it tends to create spaces between you and the athlete. You can certainly have humor in coaching—after all, we want to enjoy the pursuit of excellence when we can—it just shouldn't be at your athlete's expense. Treat your athletes how they need to be treated, give them information in a way that works best for them, the way they best receive it, as opposed to how you might want to give it. You are trying to facilitate learning and understanding, so communicating in a way that's best for the learner makes the most sense.

GUIDING PRINCIPLES AND BEHAVIORS

Feedback

There has been over a century of research on feedback and its many and varied forms. We are not going to cover it all here, but we will speak to the major considerations for feedback in sports skill learning. In sports, the primary areas of interest are the type of feedback, the frequency with which it is given, and the attentional focus of the athlete. The most important thing to consider, though, is this: the athlete is the most important source of feedback and the best learning mechanism they have.

It's their body, they control it, and they can learn how to assess their performance and correct it or repeat it. As coaches, our job should be to help create an awareness within the athlete of the required task and its application. Like all things in teaching and coaching, skill acquisition and application is not algorithmic. The same inputs seldom lead to the same outputs, so it is up to us to apply the research in this area in a way that works best for the athlete. The principles should guide our methods, but their application could vary—because people are different.

Feedback can be task-intrinsic or -extrinsic, that is to say, we can get feedback from our own experience, how we sense or feel something, or we can get feedback from an extrinsic, or external, source such as a coach or video. Extrinsic feedback (also known as augmented feedback because it provides information in addition to the intrinsic feedback) is separated into two main types: one is called KR (knowledge of result); and the other is KP (knowledge of process).

KR describes the outcome of the action, what happened, and any information connected to that result: the golf ball cut right and landed in the rough or the ball flew straight and landed on the green. KP describes the movement process that produced the action: the ball cut right because you turned your hips too soon, or you didn't get your hands through at contact, or something similar. It can be descriptive: this is the inefficiency you had in that movement; or prescriptive: this is the inefficiency, and this is what you should do to correct it. It could involve watching video of an action, or even manually moving the athlete through the desired motion. The feedback can be concurrent, given while the athlete is performing the movement or action, or terminal, given after the movement or action is competed. Lastly, the feedback can be quantitative, for example, you threw the pitch 95 mph; or qualitative, for example, your arm angle was lower on that pitch, or your stride length was shorter.

The type of feedback is important, but the frequency matters as well. Research has found that too much feedback can inhibit learning in a number of ways. A type of co-dependency is created between the athlete and the coach, in which the athlete relies exclusively on the coach for information and validation. The athlete cannot make the right choice at the right time because they have not been empowered to do so.

Too much feedback can also send the learner into cognitive overload; remember, our brains have a limited capacity to process information, and you don't want the athlete worrying so much about the feedback that they cannot focus on the task at hand. And as they say about performance, when you're thinking, you're stinking.

Another mechanism for stunted learning can occur when the athlete is trying so hard to make the desired changes that they end up making short-term changes to please the coach so they will change or stop the feedback they are receiving. They athlete might change the feedback but not build the long-term synaptic pathways that are related to the required skill. The short-term goal to change or stop the feedback is driving the change, not the long-term task goal, and the quick fix actually slows their development.

If praise is more effective than punishment, relative to learner engagement, we need to consider this when giving feedback. Often, feedback will be seen as a negative statement (remember our brain's negative bias?) about an athlete's movement and will be interpreted as a personal affront instead of objective information. The inefficiency is seen as a deficiency, that somehow the athlete is at fault or insufficient, instead of just being unskilled. The grass is green; the sky is blue; and your foot needs to be in this position, instead of that position. It can be that simple. Your athletes will want to assign an emotion to that feedback, but remember: don't get angry, get better. The emotion doesn't help, and the sooner you can help them see feedback as simply information that can help them improve, the more efficient and effective the learning will be.

In terms of frequency, early research (going back to the 1930s) suggested that more was more, that if some feedback facilitated some learning, more feedback should facilitate more learning. This did not hold true, learning was degraded when feedback was given after every repetition, often due to cognitive overload, dependency, or the resulting shift in focus from completing the task to altering the feedback.

Gabriele Wulf's research on attention and motor skill learning showed that when attentional focus was directed, through keys and subsequent feedback, to an external cue (something related to the movement effect) as opposed to an internal cue (something related to the body part or parts executing the movement), learning and retention improved.

She also tested the effect of feedback frequency under these internal- and external-cue conditions and found that when internal cues and feedback were used, less was more. Feedback given on every third practice repetition led to better learning than the same type of feedback given on every practice repetition. Having the athlete focus their attention on an internal cue with constant feedback was more detrimental to learning.

When the researchers used external cues, the frequency of feedback did not seem to be as important. Feedback given at a frequency of 33 percent or 100 percent did not seem to adversely influence learning. The external focus seemed to be the factor that was influencing learning and performance the most, not the feedback frequency. This suggests that, by creating external cues (keys and feedback that speak to the effect of the desired movement), you can give feedback at the rate the learner might need, based on their skill level, and not negatively influence that athlete's learning.

As I stated earlier, the athlete is the most important feedback mechanism they have. Intrinsic feedback can occur with an internal or external cue. Coaches are a primary source of extrinsic information to the athlete; they offer instruction and feedback as well. Another form of extrinsic feedback would be video. You could have the athlete watching themselves perform the skill, or you can watch someone else executing the desired skill efficiently or at the desired level of execution. Video is often used for post-practice or post-repetition feedback, but it can also be a powerful pre-practice or pre-repetition primer. Seeing how we want the skill performed can help the athlete formulate or revise a schema and focus their intent for the next repetition as well.

When considering external cues, we have already discussed how that could look in terms of our skill keys and subsequent feedback. There are other ways to facilitate learning externally: establishing field-of-play constraints (making the space smaller or bigger); adding lines for base positions or lanes to move in; or creating targets on the field of play, are all ways we can externally help the learner connect the skill-learning process to the outcome.

Lastly, let's talk about the delivery of your feedback, that is, your tone of voice. Feedback should be given in a measured, conversational tone. It should not be screamed or yelled, punitive or demeaning. It should be direct and honest, and I would strongly suggest that you stay clear of sarcasm. It just creates too many spaces, and we're trying to be efficient here.

What about coaches who yell a lot? I know some coaches like to yell, but again, when it comes to raising your voice, I think less is more. Your athletes will soon tune out the constant noise, and if you're yelling about everything, it's hard for them to figure out what's really important, because not every single word you say can be REALLY IMPORTANT!

I will sometimes yell at practice, because it is warranted, and it's usually connected to a lack of effort or attention to the task at hand. It is seldom about outcomes, and it's never personal. When I yell, I am confident that I will have our athletes' attention, because it doesn't happen very often. They listen, but again, raising your voice is a tool in the coaching tool kit that can produce a short-term effect. It is not an effective method for long-term change.

Teach to the Relevant Key

The idea of teaching exclusively to the key that you are working on is critical to efficient learning. The singular focus this affords allows the athlete to learn what is required more quickly. Talking about multiple keys while supposedly working on one just muddies the water. The athlete's focus is distracted, and the required task becomes unclear.

Most coaches tend to over-coach. They want to share all the information they have pertaining to a skill instead of just giving feedback and instruction relative to the specific key that they are working on. Our brains have a limited capacity to process information, so a lot of what the coach might be saying is soon lost on the athletes. As much as they might love to hear the coach's discourse on the benefits of the 4-4-3 formation in soccer versus the 4-4-2 diamond formation, they probably will have tuned them out after the first two minutes. The other 28 minutes of pontification might benefit the coach's ego, but that's about it. Teach at the pace of the learner, regardless of how expansive your knowledge is.

Goals for Drills

When devising drill constructs, there should be considerable thought given to the purpose of the drill. What skills or systems are we trying to teach here? What behaviors are we trying to reinforce? To that end, drills can be designed and constrained to force or incentivize your athletes to work on certain skills or systems, as well as maximizing transfer, opportunities to respond, and opportunities for feedback.

Competition

Competing in practice is a great extrinsic motivator. Our athletes' work-rate, engagement, and enjoyment will increase once we start keeping score. By competing and keeping objective performance data in practice, as well as in contests, we can increase the level of performance, engagement, and rate of change.

The common take on teams is that they develop chemistry through social connection. I've found that the best teams evolve and unify through the work itself, and one of the major mechanisms for this process is competition. Parts of practice, or even entire practices should focus on competing and helping our athletes learn how to engage in, and manage, the battle. As much as we want to believe that we will rise to the occasion in the big moments of competition, most often we will fall to our base level of mastery, our strongest habits. So we have to make sure that even our bad habits are good habits. We have also said that experience is the best teacher, so the more opportunities we have to compete, the better we can get at competing. Those moments of competition—the match, the game, or the race—are the most important and valuable opportunities for learning that we get.

On all the teams that I have worked with, I have never promised athletes starting positions or playing time. I do promise them that I'll invest completely in their development, but they have to earn the right to play, and everyone can earn that right. The power of the meritocracy is real. An athlete might think, *I know I'm not going to start this weekend, so there's not much incentive for me to work hard today*. Nor is there much incentive for the player promised a starting position. However, if it's possible, by working hard and getting better, to beat out the starter in practice and earn the right to play, that player's level of engagement, intention, and work will increase, and the starting player can't be complacent anymore, either; they will have to work harder, too!

This idea of teammates competing with and against each other for their mutual benefit, and the team's benefit, is called *co-opetition*. It's a term that's been around since the early 1900s and has mainly been applied in business or game theory. But it applies in sports as well and can drive significant improvement on teams. Framing the meritocracy within the team this way makes it seem more collaborative than competitive: the best thing my teammate can do for me is to try and beat me, and that's also the best thing I can do for them. Through co-opetition, individual and team skill and system weaknesses will be exposed, and those are important opportunities for learning and improvement. To paraphrase a creed attributed to the Spartan warriors, it's better to sweat (and learn) in practice than it is to bleed in battle. In simpler terms, competing in practice will help you compete more effectively in the contest.

Testing

We need to track performance to see if we are actually effecting any change, and testing the athlete's ability to execute the skills they are learning supports that. Aside from tracking progress, I have found that skill testing offers another tremendous benefit to both the athlete and coach: it can lead to a much higher degree of learner intention. Invariably, the fact that athletes are going to get a score for their performance changes the way they engage with the activity.

It's difficult to gauge how much or how little someone has learned until the skill is executed in context—that is, until we see how it's performed while the sport is being played. We have to have ways to test our athletes and hold them accountable to the execution of, or to some level of application of, a key that we've deemed to be critical to the skill. We need to tie that application of keys to outcomes and assess whether those keys are, in fact, helping that athlete to become better at the skill. In other words, we have to find qualitative and quantitative ways to connect our processes to our outcomes and track them.

Designing ways to test athletes was a significant part of my conversations with Anders Ericsson. We discussed that it was not just a matter of evaluating an athlete at one particular moment in time to evaluate and document improvement; it was also a matter of determining whether or not the athlete could hold onto the change—whether the changes held over a long period of time. We needed to show both change and retention.

We know that as more layers of complexity are added to skills, people tend to regress to their strongest habits. Enduring and lasting skill acquisition is therefore about behavioral change—building new habits. We want the new skill efficiencies to become the baseline level of execution. So testing has to involve seeing how frequently the athlete can execute the new skill with the desired mechanical efficiencies in place.

In talking this through with Anders, we discussed ways to test and reinforce behaviors so they were more likely to become habits. One of the surprising benefits we quickly observed was how much more attentive the athletes were, relative to trying to execute a skill properly, when I had a clipboard in my hand. I would evaluate a certain number of repetitions in a controlled environment: You do it, and I'll grade it. The change in our athlete's attention and intention was palpable.

More important, though, is the fact that sports are contested in a random environment, at game speed, so the controlled reps should only be the first stage of testing. In the second stage, we told the athletes we would review randomly selected repetitions from our practice video of the particular skill and assess the technical efficiency of those repetitions relative to the key that we were testing. They didn't know which of the repetitions were being tested.

This intermittent schedule of assessment worked well. We didn't have the time or staff to assess every repetition in the course of play anyway, so the random sample was the only way to go. For the athletes, the prospect of getting a score on any given repetition meant they had to play the drill with the thought that their performance might be evaluated on every repetition. If they wanted to show they were making progress, they had to try to demonstrate the proper execution of the skill every time.

Stage three of the testing process was using this same random selection/video process to assess changes in skill execution during the moment of competition itself. The ultimate litmus test for change is what happens when you compete. This testing process, finding ways to track changes in skill execution and grade them in practice and in competition, was incredibly beneficial. One thing we know is that athletes are addicted to improvement, and when you can connect process and outcome more clearly, the work rate and intention to learn and improve increase.

Data

Extrinsic feedback can also be given through statistical data. Keeping track of the numerical outcomes and giving that information to athletes and coaches can be a powerful tool for feedback and decision-making. In practice, finding ways to measure variables such as speed, power, accuracy, reaction time, or movement time can provide valuable feedback and help connect the learning process to the outcomes.

Another way to use data as feedback is to track performance outcomes when the desired skill efficiency is in place against the performance outcomes when the skill is executed inefficiently. I call this "process data," and while it is labor intensive, it can be very effective. Showing an athlete that they performed the desired skill 20 percent more effectively with the desired efficiency in place, and that their performance was diminished with the inefficiency in place, provides great feedback and significant incentive for the athlete to make and retain the desired change.

In terms of our perception of performance, there's a quote in Michael Lewis's book *Moneyball* that speaks to our inability to differentiate our perception from the reality. The book is about baseball, and he wrote, "One absolutely cannot tell, by watching, the difference between a .300 [batting average] hitter and a .275 hitter. The difference is one hit every two weeks." We need to get past how we feel about a performance, which can often be influenced by our negative bias, and see what actually happened. I've coached many athletes who had thought poorly of their performance, and yet, we'd not only won the contest but, statistically, they'd performed very well. Data is great, accurate, honest, feedback.

COLUMN 5

	5
ATHLETE RESPONSIBILITIES	• Modify or repeat goal/ schema steps (using Column 1 and Column 2) • Identify changes for next skill attempt
COACH RESPONSIBILITIES	• Help determine appropriate skill modification or progression (using Column 1 and Column 2)
GUIDING PRINCIPLES AND BEHAVIORS	• Refer to goal and skill schema columns (Column 1 and Column 2)

ATHLETE RESPONSIBILITIES

After you have attempted the skill and processed the internal and external feedback you've received, you need to commit to an intention for the next repetition. If you executed the skill or skill key correctly, you should try to repeat it to see if the change was lightning in a bottle, or if there was a real shift in skill execution that occurred. When you can consistently demonstrate that the desired change has happened, you can shift your attentional focus to the next part of the key, the next key, or the next task goal. If there was an inefficiency, you need to determine what you will do differently on the next repetition. These decisions don't have to happen in a vacuum—your coach plays a role in this, too—but once the appropriate modification has been identified, you need to form the appropriate modified schema in your mind and prepare to execute the next repetition.

COACH RESPONSIBILITIES

You are helping the athlete to determine appropriate modifications or progressions. The athlete attempts the skill, and you've given them feedback on the technical efficiencies or inefficiencies they've displayed. Remember, it is important to give feedback to both. You need to assess the first skill attempt and determine, based on the level of execution, the progress the athlete has made toward achieving the daily goal and the task goal. Ask yourself what adjustments or modifications should be made for the next attempt and communicate them. If the athlete has demonstrated a sufficient level of execution, you should progress to the next skill key. Coach and teach to what is: you have to operate in truth but continue to find ways to catch them doing it right. Praise any and all parts of the skill that were performed correctly and give information in a way that's best for the learner regarding any inefficiencies, so that the athlete can have the best possible chance of a correct response on the next attempt.

COLUMN 6

	6
ATHLETE RESPONSIBILITIES	• Repeat skill attempt (using Columns 3, 4, and 5) *or* • Attempt skill application (Column 7)
COACH RESPONSIBILITIES	• Repeat skill teaching (using Columns 3, 4, and 5) *or* • Move to skill coaching (Column 7)
GUIDING PRINCIPLES AND BEHAVIORS	• Utilize all previous skill acquisition principles/ behaviors (Columns 1-6) *or* • Move to skill application principles/behaviors (Column 7)

ATHLETE RESPONSIBILITY

Your job is to reset and bring the right effort and intention to the next skill attempt using the sequence of events outlined in columns 3, 4, and 5. After the skill attempt, your coach will have you repeat the acquisition process to add more layers of skill, or move to Column 7 and try to apply the skill in competition. That competition could be in practice, but it could also be that your time to learn is done and now it's time to compete against an opponent.

COACH RESPONSIBILITY

Keep teaching and coaching within the framework. Maximize transfer, opportunities to respond, and opportunities for feedback. For example, if the key 1 skill part is in place, you should be giving most of your feedback to key 2. But, if necessary, you can still refer to key 1. Coach to the relevant keys and teach at the pace of the learner. If the athlete needs to repeat the attempt under the same conditions, or repeat the attempt under modified conditions due to a change in skill execution, move to Column 5.

Once a sufficient level of skill has been demonstrated, move to Column 7 and try to help the athlete apply that skill through competition in practice. You might, due to time constraints, have to help them apply their skills in an actual contest as well.

GUIDING PRINCIPLES AND BEHAVIORS

Continue to apply the guiding principles and behaviors outlined in Columns 1–6. Either the athlete will have achieved the required level or skill acquisition, or they will have made as much change as possible relative to the constraints placed upon them (such as time). Then they move to Column 7 and apply what they've learned to the moment of competition.

COLUMN 7

	7
ATHLETE RESPONSIBILITIES	• Apply skill • Set and enact competitive intent • Compensate and adjust
COACH RESPONSIBILITIES	• Systems and tactics pre-/during competition • Coach the athlete • Review
GUIDING PRINCIPLES AND BEHAVIORS	• Specialization • Emotional control • Decision-making • Best effort • Mental focus

ATHLETE RESPONSIBILITIES

Competing in sports is a physical contest that demands controlled and intense mental focus and physical effort. The moment of competition starts well before the event. Sleep, recovery modalities (heat, ice, compression, and so on), nutrition/fueling, hydration, and physical and mental well-being are all factors that you should consider leading into competition. Planning and preparation are important parts of competitive excellence as well. We will discuss these further in Part III of the book.

The athlete's responsibility in this process is to work, learn, and compete, and skill application is a big part of this competition phase. The athletes now have to apply the physical, mental, and social skills they have developed, as well as the technical skills and systems they have learned in practice, to the moment of competition.

Athletes need to bring an intention to the moment of competition. I said earlier that skill confidence is connected to skill competence, and this is the moment where that matters the most. All the hours of practice the athletes invest are to prepare them to compete, and that competitive intent is expressed through their skill, decision-making, emotional control, discipline, effort, and, in team sports, their ability to be a great teammate. It's tempting to view competition exclusively through the lens of outcome and focus only on winning, but the athlete needs to resist that temptation and focus on the things they must do, in the order they must do them, to give themselves the best chance of achieving the outcome they want. It's play to play, point to point, pitch to pitch. Focus on controlling all the things you can in these moments, commit to good process, and the results tend to take care of themselves.

Competitive intent is also connected to perspective. Are we playing to win? Or are we playing not to lose? There's a big difference here, and it's linked to belief and emotional control. Playing to win is assertive (I prefer this word to *aggressive* because it's an intention, not an emotion). The athletes are connected and unified. Playing not to lose is a completely different energy. It's anxious and passive. We're back to hoping that the outcome will be favorable instead of knowing what we can or have to do in order to give ourselves the best possible chance of achieving that favorable outcome.

So much of how athletes compete is connected to belief and intent. Statements that express that intent, such as "I can" or "I will," lead to conviction and action. When it is difficult to compete—and it always gets difficult at some point—you should focus on what you can do, the things you can control, and put your energy into doing those things to the best of your ability.

In terms of controllable elements, we talk to our athletes about a number things, notably Es (effort, energy, execution, edge) and Cs (communication, connection, control, celebration, consistency). We have also talked about positive thought, positive action, and positive emotion—whatever mechanisms we can devise that help connect the athlete to their competitive intention.

As the contest ensues, the competitive environment might change. For outdoor sports that could be the weather, or the track conditions, something to do with the physical constraints of the activity. There will also be in-contest tactical changes that occur, such as different matchups or different systems. These tactical changes are geared toward exploiting a weakness or playing to a strength. The athlete's ability to identify the changes and then adjust to them in a timely fashion is an important part of competitive excellence. Competing to "what is" as opposed to what you want or what you expect will be much more productive. Being able to compensate and adjust is an important part of competitive success.

COACH RESPONSIBILITIES

We have our team's skills and systems in place, so now we have to prepare for the moment of competition. Having the best chance of competitive success starts with a plan. What tactics will you employ? What opponent patterns or weaknesses can you exploit or leverage to your advantage? When it comes to scouting, simple observation and data collection can help anyone create a solid game plan because all teams and all athletes have patterns. While it's important to identify and to play to your opponent's weaknesses, I think it's equally, if not more, important to play to your strengths. Also remember that the contest is going to be won or lost on the field of play, not on paper. So don't try to do things tactically that your athletes can't do technically, and for all of the reasons we've previously discussed about cognitive capacity and knowing your audience, resist the temptation to over-coach. The plan won't be good if it's not understood, and if the athletes can't understand the plan, they certainly won't be able to apply it in the contest.

In the moment of competition, we absolutely need to make in-contest tactical or technical adjustments. If there are opponent weaknesses you can exploit to your advantage, you should, and as your opponent compensates and adjusts to your tactics, you'll have to do the same in return. If the plan isn't working, resist the temptation to deflect responsibility by yelling at your athletes. Standing on the sideline berating or belittling athletes about the last play does little to help the athlete or the team prepare for the next one. The athletes shouldn't feel like they have to battle you and the opponent. Throwing your arms up in the air after a mistake, rolling your eyes, or generally deflecting bad outcomes onto your athletes is self-indulgent and immature. In-contest tactical adjustments need to happen, but that should be a rational discussion, not an emotional one.

Coaches who indulge in this type of behavior generally want all of the credit for the good outcomes and none of the responsibility for the bad ones. It should be the other way around: the athletes are the ones doing the work; they deserve the kudos when things go well. When the team comes up short, it's on you. As the great John Wooden said, "If they haven't learned, you haven't taught." It's not their fault they can't do what you're asking them to do—it's yours. You are there to help your athletes manage the moment of competition and maximize their chances of competitive success. You can be frustrated if the contest is not going well, sure, but try to be the adult in the room and channel that energy into helping your athletes win the next play instead of yelling at them, or the officials, about the last one. The pursuit of competitive excellence is demanding, but it should never be demeaning.

I think that in youth sports fundamental skills tend to be neglected in lieu of systems—systems that are often far beyond what's required to succeed at that level. What is required at the youth sports level (and every level, in fact) is the ability to execute the fundamental skills of the sport. Coaches tend to focus on systems or tactics because they are easier to teach, and consequently the amount of over-coaching in youth sports is significant. The coach is so intent on showing how much they know about the systems and intricacies of the sport that they don't do right by the people they are supposed to serve. The systems might be great, but if the athletes lack the level of fundamental mastery required to execute them, they are of no use. Again, don't try to do things tactically that your athletes can't do technically and, more importantly, teach the fundamental skills first and then build into their application.

As I've said, the coach sets the temperature in the room, whether they want to or not. If they're anxious about competing, their athletes will likely be anxious, too. If they're relaxed, the athletes will relax. If the goal of the competition is to win, and we know that emotion can move people into an irrational space as opposed to a rational one, we should be very careful about how we use emotion in our coaching. Your emotions needn't be the team's emotions; again, control yourself and help your athletes to compete with composure.

In my current coaching job, many people have commented about my calm or stoic demeanor on the sideline during our matches. I am not indifferent or ambivalent about the moment of competition. In fact, I care deeply about it, but I choose to coach to the moment. We happen to play in a venue that sells out. There are 6,000 people in the arena, and there is plenty of "juice" in the building. I don't need to add to that. I try to convey a calm demeanor so that our athletes can hopefully feel a bit calmer as well. There are certainly times when I have to use emotion, I might even raise my voice occasionally. But again, that's usually a choice, a coaching decision—not a reaction.

When I coached the USA national teams, we would often be playing meaningful matches in foreign countries with fewer than 100 people in the stands. We'd be playing in cavernous stadiums with hardly any "'juice" in the building at all, other than our competitive intent. I would stand on the sideline and give instruction, celebrate successes, and generally be as loud and as energy-giving as I could. Again, this was a conscious decision. Our job as coaches is to help our athletes manage the moment of competition, and that is exactly what I was trying to do—use my influence and energy for the betterment of the team.

Lastly, when the contest is over, regardless of the outcome, you need to review the performance. We train to compete, so how we perform in the contest is the ultimate litmus test of our skill acquisition and application. The review will allow you to identify opportunities for improvement as well as chances to catch your athletes doing things "right."

Watch the film, try to get whatever lessons you can learn from that moment of competition, and move on. To that end, I suggest you review the performance sooner rather than later, but make sure you're in a rational space when you do it. Reviewing the contest in an emotional state will seldom provide the objectivity required to get the most out of this process.

The review should not just be an exercise in self-flagellation relative to skill inefficiencies or tactical errors; it should be used to reinforce and celebrate good performances as well. The temptation will be to do a deep dive after a loss and conduct a more cursory review after a win. Resist that temptation. Winning can mask a lot of problems, so always try to be objective, consistent, and thorough in your review. You and your athletes will be better for it.

GUIDING PRINCIPLES AND BEHAVIORS

Specialization

At some point in an athlete's sporting career they will have to specialize. They will have to choose a sport, an event, or a position, and commit to pursuing competitive excellence in that chosen athletic domain. Often, though, athletes will be pushed to specialize too early.

In youth sports, early specialization tends to manifest itself in a couple of ways. One is the pressure to play one sport exclusively at an early age. This is usually driven by one of two things: the first is fear ("You'll never make it to the top, or even the next level, if you don't train exclusively in this sport"); the second is scheduling ("To be on this team you have to participate in all of our activities, and by the way, we have scheduled activities from July to June)."

The other type of specialization to watch out for in youth sports is positional specialization. There is often a strong tendency to assign positions, and therefore skill sets, to younger athletes based on body type. In youth basketball, the tall athletes play forward or center, the not-so-tall athletes play guard. The guards handle the ball and shoot three-pointers while the forwards post up and shoot short-range shots. But these "athletes" might be eight years old. We don't know if they'll be tall or small as adults, let alone who the best ball handler or rebounder might be.

I think it would be best if everyone was taught all of the fundamental skills of the game and that everyone played most, if not all, of the positions. Of course, playing like this might not be best for the coach's win-loss record, but it is absolutely best for the physical and mental development of the athletes. We've all heard of the tall youth basketball player who never gets to handle the ball in youth sports, who then gets to high school and stops growing. Maybe they're 5'11" and the coach wants them to play point guard, but they have no ball-handling ability, only because they were taller than the other kids when they were younger. The athlete's physical attributes seem to fit the position, but their skills are not even close, and as most of us know, learning later in life is not easier than learning earlier. What a travesty!

To illustrate the value of having all of your athletes learn all of the fundamental skills, we should discuss the concept of generalized specialists—people who are good at all of the skills of their sport, but are great at two or three things specific to their position. In volleyball, there are five specialized positions, one of which is the *setter*. This person is responsible for most of the second contacts in rallies as they set the ball for the *hitters* so they can spike it and try to score. Another specialized position is *middle blocker*. This person primarily attacks fast-tempo sets and is responsible for blocking the opponent's hitters. They block starting from the middle of the court so they can defend the whole net, hence the name. Middles are not setters; they are generally tall and are known to have functional ball-control skills, but ball control is seldom their forte. With our 2008 team, we taught our middles (as well as every other player on the team) how to set. In the Olympic final, at match point, one of our middle blockers set the ball that was spiked to win the match. It was a broken play, and it was a big moment. The middle stepped in, set a very hittable ball, and the rest is history. If we had trained him exclusively to his positional skills, he would not have been as composed, confident, or capable, and who knows what might have happened? What we do know is this, we won the gold medal, and a middle blocker set the ball that won the match. It is important to develop generalized specialists.

There is also scientific evidence that suggests that specializing in one sport too early in your athletic career limits how good you can become in that sport. The early specialization becomes a limiting factor. In his book, *Range: Why Generalists Triumph in a Specialized World*, investigative reporter David Epstein suggests (and his opinion is substantiated by empirical research) that we should have our young athletes play as many sports as they can, for as long as they can, before they choose the one they wish to pursue exclusively.[30] Young athletes who participate in a variety of sports have a better chance of excelling in the sport they eventually choose.

Emotional Control

Just as effective practices start with an intention to learn, you should approach the moment of competition with an intention to say and do everything you can to help your team win. Learning the skills required to help you and your teammates do that is important. These aren't just skills in the physical realm, though; emotional control is also a big part of consistent competitive success.

We will have emotions when we compete, but we don't have to succumb to them. Positive emotion is great, but it's the roller coaster of negative emotion we need to watch out for. Fear, anger, and frustration seldom lead to greatness.

Instead of emotion, I like to talk to athletes about creating energy, an effort and intention that we can control. Creating energy through our actions, such as physical contact, communication, celebration, and expressed competitive intent, can help teams stay connected and focused through the inevitable ebbs and flows of the contest. Emotion is part of the human condition, it can be positive or negative, and while you should encourage positive emotion, we have to learn to manage the negative. We cannot replace emotion, but we can learn to control it and channel it.

Teaching and coaching to emotional control is not very common. In fact, most coaches are trying to create emotion, but that pursuit can lead to some significant inconsistencies in performance. There are lots of reasons we should teach emotional control to our athletes, but you can only learn it by being put in uncomfortable situations and then, through experience and feedback, figure out how to manage those moments of adversity.

Dr. Ken Ravizza would say that you can always respond to the response. That the emotion doesn't have to control the action. This idea of learning to control our emotional responses was also investigated by Dr. Steve Peters in his book, *The Chimp Paradox*. Peters uses the analogy of two brains—one human and one chimp—to describe the interaction between emotion and rational thought. The human brain is our prefrontal cortex, which is responsible for rational thought (think organization and focus), and the chimp brain is our limbic system, which is responsible for our emotions and our base behaviors (such as the fight-or-flight response, behaviors we can influence but not control). He also uses the analogy of a computer in our brain, a system that advises the human brain and the chimp based on prior knowledge and experience.[31]

I have found that most people are not aware of our limbic systems or the prefrontal cortex, or their respective roles relative to emotional response and rational thought. Once you talk to them about these structures, though, there is a great opportunity to teach to emotional control. Earlier, I said that our athletes should not get angry; they should get better. You can see that what is being said here is don't "go limbic," stay in that rational prefrontal cortex space, because going limbic means you will become irrational and impede the learning or competing process.

Peters's book also speaks to the very important and freeing idea that our limbic responses do not have to define us. An emotionally driven or irrational thought does not define who we are, it is just a thought that we can choose to act on or let disappear into the ether. This is incredibly freeing for people. Our actions define us, not our thoughts. A person can have a bad thought, but that doesn't mean they are a bad person. If that bad thought leads to bad actions? Well, that's another story.

Applying this to sports, an athlete makes a mistake and that leads to a negative thought. The athlete can create a space between that negative thought and their next action (taking a breath is a good mechanism for this). In that space, they can validate the thought or ignore it, but they get to choose the subsequent action. They can be curious about the thought, but they do not have to succumb to it. In more concrete terms, a mistake happens, and the athlete thinks, *I'm terrible.* They can pause and look at that statement, *Am I really terrible? No, I'm actually not. I'm quite good!* And then they can choose to act accordingly. They could reflect on the thought: *Why did I think that particular thought after that mistake? How could I respond to that mistake differently next time?* Or: *That was weird. Oh, well, back to the task at hand.* You can respond to the response!

The last thing to note about emotional control is that emotions can spread from person to person. They can be contagious, and so another real benefit of emotional control is that it not only keeps the athlete present and engaged, it can also help to keep the team present and engaged. Research has shown that high-intensity emotions, such as anger or fear, tend to spread more quickly and have a large effect on others. Conversely, maintaining a cool, calm demeanor can influence others as well. We all have a focus of control—that's ourselves—but our sphere of influence might be vast. The ripples, especially from our emotional outbursts, might spread far and fast, so we should control ourselves, not just to control our performance, but the performance of our athletes and teams as well.

Interview with Riley Salmon

Riley Salmon joined Team USA in May 2001. Riley is barely 6'4", and that's with his volleyball shoes on. He competed in two Olympic Games, 2004 in Athens and 2008 in Beijing. In Beijing, he was one of the starting outside hitters on the team that won gold. Riley was a little shorter than most of his volleyball peers, and his pathway to the national team was atypical, to say the least. Riley spent a lot of years battling himself and his opponents. His relative lack of height, and the fact that he did not play D-1 college volleyball meant he spent a lot of time and energy trying to prove himself. Once he learned how to control himself and his emotions, the quality and consistency of his play was remarkable. He now coaches the men's volleyball team at Concordia University in Irvine, California.

Riles, one of the most significant changes you made, in addition to all the technical stuff, was your ability to figure out who you were out there and play to your strengths—that whole idea of controlling your emotions and how that translated into superior performance. What can you tell us about that part of your journey?

Riley Salmon: I think that for me, just making it to the level of Team USA was cumbersome. I had to overcome tons of obstacles to get there. The national team was never on my radar—ever—in my life early on. I didn't take that conventional path, as you know. [Note: traditionally, an athlete plays in a club, gets recruited to a top D-1 university, plays well at that school, becomes an All-American, and then gets invited to the national team. That was not Riley's journey.] I played two years of junior college, and I was recruited to go to a couple of universities, but I found out that school was not my strong suit. So I left and went to play on the professional beach tour for two seasons with the AVP [Association of Volleyball Professionals]. Out of the blue, I got a call to play in a tournament in Europe where our national B-team was playing. I showed up, and I thought I played really well. But I thought it was a one-and-done thing for the national team.

Then in 2001, Doug Beal, the head coach at the time, called and asked me to try out. I was probably ninth or 10th on the depth chart in my position, and they only carry four outsides on the roster for the Olympics. I didn't think I had much of a shot. I just put my head down and worked really hard. I thought I could out-compete anybody through sheer physical effort and being more aggressive. But that plan didn't work out as well as I thought it would. I quickly learned that I couldn't succeed that way. I would freak out a lot—not just at myself, but my teammates as well. I would run pretty hot.

It got to the point where I was in danger of being kicked off the team. I didn't want to be that way; it was just the only way I knew. I wanted to be better, the best version of Riley Salmon, and I kept wondering, *What does that look like?* And what that looked like was to be a much smarter volleyball player than anybody ever could have imagined, to try be the greatest teammate out there, and to encourage my teammates instead of dumping on them when they were doing bad things in practice. It sounds very simple, but it took some time. I really believe I would've never mentally matured into the gold medalist that I am today had it not been for the conversations you and I had about the importance of emotional control.

It was clear that it was an issue. I just don't think anyone presented what the solution looked like as part of a framework. It's one thing to say, "Stop doing it." But it's another thing to figure out how to do that.

After a couple of years of trying to work through some of the technical changes, it felt like it was time to address some of these other things.

RS: One of the things I can remember vividly is when you would let me get close to the emotional edge. I could play as crazy as you would let me. As soon as I would start to run hot, you would say, "You're getting too close, settle down." And I would. Obviously, that didn't happen the very first time, but eventually the process sunk in. I can remember distinctly calming down and playing a lot better. As I could control my emotions, I started to home in on my technical skills. I could concentrate more than before. I could lead and help guys around me. When I ran hot, there was no chance of that happening.

You had a drastic transformation. How did you learn to control yourself? How did that happen?

RS: The World Championships where we did miserably (2006, USA placed 10th) was a huge eye-opener for me. When you really have to be the man and you can't step up, and you let a bunch of guys down, that was extremely disappointing. I realized that my role was not to be that guy.

So I think I just took a real hard look at myself and said, "I've got to be really good at what my coach thinks I'm really good at." You gave me that list of what I needed to do. It was clear, firm rules and solid solutions. Doing that took a lot of trust, but in the end, I didn't have to be anyone else, just the best me. I just came to believe in our system, like we talked about all the time. I had to make those changes.

Before that, I tried to be good at too many things, and that was part of why I would get so angry and frustrated. There were still times when I would run hot, but the amount of that behavior kept dropping down.

You're coaching now, so I've got to ask: could you be a good coach if you were still that guy?

RS: No, I don't think I could, honestly. I couldn't do what I'm doing if I hadn't transformed as a person. I'm not burdened by that emotional load. I learned to play my best instead of having to beat myself and beat the opponent.

The short-term reward of an Olympic gold medal is cool, but the long-term reward is even better. Getting to share knowledge, teaching the game, teaching people to be good people is exactly where the reward is for me.

Decision-Making

The plan is just a starting point that is based on your opponent's history. What they choose to do against you today might be different, so you must be able to read the situation in real-time and adjust. This combination of information—what you know plus what you see gives you the opportunity to make the right choice at the right time, to make "the right play." After you commit to a course of action, an outcome will occur that will either be in your favor or your opponent's. You then take that information and apply it to the next moment of competition. You adjust, you compensate, you learn. The formula becomes:

$$\text{DECISION-MAKING} = \text{PLAN} \longrightarrow \text{READ} \longrightarrow \text{PLAY} \longrightarrow \text{LEARN}$$

Then you repeat it. The process sounds simple and logical, but its application is more nuanced than you might think. Learning to read the situation is hard to do and tough to quantify—but it's reading and seeing that sets the great ones apart from the rest of us. Reading is a premier skill in many sports. Playing to what is actually happening and then making the right choice at the right time (and having the skills required to do so) are key to consistent performance. We need to teach people to move from the guesswork of "what if" to the reality of "what is."

Best Effort

Giving best effort to achieve the outcome goal in the moment of competition is critical. We know that there are a number of elements of the competitive equation that we don't get to control, so our effort is the key to our achievement, but it also helps to frame our outcomes as well.

The idea of "best effort" is acknowledged conceptually, but it's poorly defined as a comprehensive approach to achievement; it evokes more thoughts of "trying hard" than the pursuit of excellence. However, doing your "best" is an important part of that process. It is our intention and commitment to best effort that drives our competitive process and affords us the opportunity to be at peace with ourselves when we're done. We can commit to the pursuit of significant achievement and, regardless of the outcome, be okay. If you did the best you could and lost, then you were beaten. You weren't good enough, but you tried your best, and that's all any of us can do.

If you didn't get the outcome you worked and hoped for, but you said and did everything you could to achieve it, then you can get the lessons learned and try again or move on to another goal. If you come up short and know that you did leave some meat on the bone, that there were things you could have, should have, or would have done differently, then you've opened the door to regret—and that's a tough thing to live with.

Do your best. Say and do everything you can to win the race, the match, the play, the point. You'll be good enough, or you won't, but either way you'll sleep soundly at night.

Mental Focus

Mihaly Csikszentmihalyi's concept of psychological "flow," expressed in his classic book of the same name, describes an intense state of concentration or focus that can be attained in many activities, including sports.[32] The athlete feels their best and performs their best. The athlete is so focused on the activity that they are free from distraction and free from any other thoughts other than those relevant to the task at hand, which leads to an increase in intellectual, creative, and physical performance.

For flow to occur, the task has to be challenging, but not too challenging. The optimal amount of difficulty has been determined to be +4 percent, so the challenge should require the subject to perform at a level 4 percent higher than their current skill level.

The flow state can lead to extraordinary performances. It is difficult to attain and difficult to sustain, but the performance benefits of being "in flow" are significant. It has been estimated that people are in the flow state 5–20 percent of the time, and while we should practice creating more flow, the relatively small amount of time a person experiences flow begs the question, what should we be doing the other 80–95 percent of the time?

Intense focus on a challenge that won't induce anxiety due to its difficulty or complexity, or boredom because it's too easy, can help us achieve flow. In sports, flow can happen periodically—everything seems easy and time seems to slow down. It is tough to schedule opponents that are consistently 4 percent better than you are, though. We should strive for flow, but increasing our ability to focus on the task at hand can benefit our performance in the non-flow states as well. We might not be in flow, but we can still be on-task.

Mental focus in sports, related to the athlete's ability to focus on the task at hand and the competitive environment, is important. The athlete must constantly interpret that information to help them make the right choice at the right time. It's not just about decision-making, it's about making sure we are collecting the best information we can as a basis for our decisions. To that end, what we choose to focus on, relative to our own performance cues and the actions of the opponents, matters. Mental focus can be disrupted by internal or external distractions. Examples of internal distractions would be thoughts of the last play, thinking about the next play or the outcome, fatigue, or an internal attentional focus. External distractions would be things like crowd noise, bad officiating, or the coach or an opponent yelling at the athlete.

Like most things, our ability in this area can increase with practice. The greater our ability to mentally focus, the more we'll be in control of our thoughts and actions, and it's possible our chance of reaching the flow state will increase as well. By attending to the task, or the parts of the task that we need to, we can focus on the process, free of distraction. It gives us something concrete and tangible to go to in the big moments—the plan, a decision-making cue, a skill key—something real that can help our performance. We can have emotional responses and respond to them with rational points of focus that add value to the moment of competition. As renowned major league baseball manager Joe Madden says, "There is no fear in the process." Our mental focus keeps us in a rational space and stops us from going limbic.

Focusing requires energy, and athletes, like everyone else, do not have unlimited supplies of that. The ability to focus is critical, but the idea that we are going to be *focused* for the entire duration of the competition is unrealistic. We have to learn to bring our attention to the moments of competition and, between plays, step back, maybe take a breath and then, when the next play is about to begin, reset and reengage our focus. Ken Ravizza would talk to athletes often about this idea of stepping in (focusing) and then stepping out (taking a breath to reset) to sustain the level of mental focus required for elite competition. This intermittent strategy is the only way you can stay focused and on-task for prolonged periods of time.

PART III

Achievement

Part II supported the skill acquisition and skill application required to achieve your goals. But there's more work to do; there are other factors to consider in the pursuit of significant achievement. In this section, we will discuss other elements critical to the process of competitive excellence and show how they intersect to create powerful synergies.

When you choose to live in the competitive arena, you quickly learn that the margins between winning and losing can be small. Winning feels much better, but losing comes with the territory—it's an occupational hazard. The higher the level you coach, the thinner the margins become. Seasons and quadrennials will be defined by a few plays in a few key moments of a few key contests. To give yourself the best chance of success in those moments, you have to plan and prepare for them from the start. Accepting and normalizing the reality of competition goes a long way in helping you and your athletes feel prepared for when it gets big. And at some point, it's absolutely going to get big. Your ability to compete with composure in those moments, to be present, to be in control, and to say and do everything you can to help yourself and/or your team win is critical to competitive success. You'll be good enough or you won't, but either way you'll know you did everything you could.

7

Trust

The path to competitive excellence and achievement begins with trust, the currency that makes high-functioning teams work. Trust is defined as a firm belief in the reliability, truth, ability, or strength of someone or something. The tough thing with trust is that it takes a long time to build and you can lose it in a second, but you absolutely need it to succeed. I believe that trust should be developed and nurtured in three different ways. First, the athlete must learn to trust themselves. Second, for athletes who play team sports, they have to learn to trust their teammates. Third, athletes need to be able to trust their coaches. If trust can be developed in these three areas, learning will improve and so will the ability to compete. Trust increases the chances of achieving the outcome goal.

TRUST YOURSELF

Trusting yourself starts with trusting your motives and goals. Is this what I really want to do? Is that where I really want to be? Am I willing to invest the required time and energy into this endeavor? Feeling like you're "where you're supposed to be," doing "what you're supposed to be doing" is important. The work is hard enough without wondering why you are doing it.

Self-trust is also connected to being trustworthy. Character off the field of play tends to lead to character on it. Are you consistent and true in your words and actions? To others and to yourself?

Next the athlete has to learn to trust their fundamental skills. Do they have the required technical efficiencies in place? Can they execute them at the required levels? Then the athlete has to trust their ability to apply those skills in the moment of competition. Can they read the situation, attend to and process the right information, and not only make the right choice at the right time but execute the skill correctly in that moment as well? When they're out there competing, they need to know that they have what it takes to succeed. No one wants to be out there hoping they're good enough.

Lastly, can the athlete trust their emotional control, can they trust they will be present and ready to say and do everything they can to succeed? Free of the last play, or the next one, or the screaming fan, or the trash-talking opponent. Can they trust that, in the big moments, they can control themselves so they can control their performance? Critical to building self-trust is the commitment to doing the work and learning from the mistakes. As John Wooden said, "You earn the right to be proud and confident." Having all these things in place—motives, character, skill competence, and skill confidence—builds self-trust.

TRUST YOUR TEAMMATES

No one in team sports can be successful alone, and yet some people tend to think of teammates as merely "the other people that play on my team." It's a limiting perspective, to say the least, but it does speak to a missed opportunity on teams. Being a teammate is an important responsibility, and there are significant synergies that are created when team members trust each other. It affords the opportunity to move your team from functional, where people show up and play, to high-functioning, where there's clarity of purpose, intent, and authentic connection leading to optimal performance and achievement. High-functioning teams are great to be a part of, and once people have been on teams that are high-functioning and they learn how those teams work, connect, and communicate, they'll want to experience that feeling of unity and shared purpose again. They'll have learned how high-functioning teams feel and function, and they can go off and create their own. It's a gift that keeps on giving.

Teammate interaction is another opportunity on teams. A lot of athletes join teams without having a clear understanding of what the boundaries for action and interaction should be. On teams where friendship is demanded, fake friendship might develop because teammates feel compelled or are instructed to go through the emotional motions. People giving teammates high fives and putting their arms around each other in a timeout doesn't necessarily build genuine friendship, or—what teams really need—trust. For trust to evolve, these actions and interactions should be authentic and organic, not demanded or required, and come from a place of genuine care and concern for the team and the people on it.

In my experience, these authentic connections between teammates are better developed and strengthened through "work" than they are through "play." Not that social interaction doesn't help, it just shouldn't be a requirement. These connections lead to trust, and trust lends maximum efficiency to the process of individually and collectively achieving the goal. Trusting there is a shared agenda to achieve a significant outcome means a group will have no reservations about consistently bringing their best efforts and intentions to each practice and competition. They may not necessarily want to see each other outside of team activities, though, and that's fine.

Contrary to popular belief, a team is not a family. Families have to accept and tolerate dysfunction from time to time because of their inherent genetic obligation. High-functioning teams have great teammates who have earned both the right to be there and their teammates' trust.

Having a framework in place for teammate actions and interactions gives athletes guidance and clarity. It provides boundaries relative to the expectations around these important relationships. I tell our athletes this often: you only get to be teammates for a short time; you can be friends for the rest of your lives. Being a teammate is a much more important responsibility, and to help athletes fulfill that responsibility, I use the following guidelines for teammate behavior:

- **Friendly, without the pressure to become friends**
  This doesn't mean you can't be friends, and it certainly doesn't mean you shouldn't be friends with your teammates. However, it's unlikely that you'll have 50 best friends on the football team, and that's okay. If the expectation is friendship, you'll get faux friendship because we can't have 50 best friends every season. You can be friendly to those 50, though. You can invest in those relationships in a way that is authentic and that helps the team, and that in turn allows trust to evolve. You will probably have friends on your teams; this idea of "friendly" just takes the pressure off forcing that process, and on the off chance that you don't particularly like someone on the team, you can still be a great teammate.

  We all like to be liked, but having that be the driving force in your relationships, especially on teams, means you are giving others the power to define you. You act to please them, so their expectation of your behavior drives your behavior. You should be accepted for who you are, not for who people want you to be. To that end, I think it is more important for teammates to be respected than liked. You shouldn't "work" for the people on your team, trying to earn their acceptance and approval. You should work with them to achieve something significant.

Also, there are times when teammates will have to have difficult or uncomfortable conversations. Concern over being judged by, or hurting the feelings of, your friends can be a barrier to honest and direct communication. Being a teammate allows you to operate in truth, with genuine concern for the team and the teammate, but without concern for any potential collateral damage to a friendship.

- **Inclusive to all teammates; there's only one cool clique, the team!**
  When you're on a team you want to unify, not fracture. Cliques create silos, and silos create agendas. Connect and include your teammates in activities. If they choose to join, great, if they don't, no problem, but always make the effort to include and connect.

- **Be respectful**
  You should try to learn about your teammates' lives outside of the field of play. Their likes and dislikes, their family life, where they're from, their experiences. Things that can help you understand more about that person and help you to develop respect and empathy. Once you can understand more about a teammate off the field of play, it helps you understand them more on it.

- **Loyal to the team and the people on it**
  If you want to develop trust, you need to be loyal. Your allegiance should be to the team and the people on it.

- **Genuine care and concern for each other**
  While you might not be best friends with everyone on the team, you can have genuine care and concern for your teammates. These are the people who are going to help you achieve the outcome goal. You should care about them because your lives are now inextricably connected. This is the only iteration of this team that is ever going to be. You should want your teammates to be in a happy and healthy space; so checking in, offering your help or support are things you should want to do to help your team and your teammates.

- **Forgive and learn**
  Teammates will make mistakes. Once the consequence for the transgression has been enacted, we have to forgive our teammate, learn from the experience, and move on. I'm not a fan of forgive and forget, because that presents the opportunity for the same mistake to happen again. Forgive and learn, though? Absolutely. It's a critical part of competitive excellence. But remember, you are also a teammate. So it's not just about "forgive and learn" for others, you have to be able to "forgive and learn" for yourself as well.

- **Communicating honestly and directly**
  Honest and direct communication is not mean. You should communicate with genuine care and concern but also communicate to be understood. Make sure there are no spaces between what you say and what's heard or understood, because those spaces will be filled with assumptions instead of the information you were trying to convey. Listen to understand as well. There's a tendency to listen to reply, but communication is not about winning and losing conversations, it's about sharing

information and understanding. Coaches might consider an acknowledgment rule to make sure people are heard, or ask the athlete some questions to make sure the message is understood.

- **Earned accountability**

  If you live the process of competitive excellence, you work, learn, compete, and are a great teammate, then you can earn the right, through the quality and consistency of your actions, to hold other teammates to the team's standards of excellence. You don't have to be the best player, or have the best outcomes, but if you consistently commit to best process, you can and should speak with genuine care and concern to teammates who are not honoring their commitment to the team's goals.

Embracing these teammate "guiding principles" helps with learning, achievement, enjoyment, and trust. They give you the opportunity to operate in truth and add value to the team and the people on it. I try to make it clear very early in our athletes' training that their improvement helps us improve; a better "U" makes a better "Us." Once players internalize that lesson, they learn to see improvement and team-oriented behavior as a win-win, that every step closer they come to excellence is a step toward achieving the significant outcomes the team has committed to. The rising tide lifts all boats.

Another important teammate quality is the powerful and selfless act of helping your teammates. In fact, in sports, it's often said that the great ones make those around them better. We seldom teach to that or reward it. But we love it when we have an athlete who connects the team and elevates the performance of their teammates. The common goal for most people is to be the best person on the team, but what if we could better express and appreciate the value of being the best person for the team? Selflessness, being prepared to add value through your actions, or by supporting the actions of another, to help the team achieve the goal, is an important part of being a great teammate.

Interview with Scott Touzinsky

Scott Touzinsky tore his anterior cruciate ligament (ACL) in 2004 and was told he'd probably never play professional volleyball again. Four years later, he helped Team USA capture gold at the Beijing Olympics. Scott made the team in January 2008; the Olympics were in August. He was a late but very important addition. Scott could play the game well, but his value as a teammate was as important as his role as fourth outside hitter (of four). He is an Olympian, he is a gold medalist, and he absolutely helped the team accomplish that, even though his on-court contributions in the Games were less significant than those of others.

———

Scott, your influence on the 2008 team was profound, even though your role as a fourth outside hitter was not terribly exciting. You weren't a star on an Olympic gold-medal-winning team, but you were a gold-medal teammate. You played a key role in our success. Your actions had a profound, positive influence on the group.

Scott Touzinsky: For me, the role didn't really matter, I was just stoked to be on the team. Better to be on the roster as the fourth outside hitter than sitting at home as the fifth, right? And that was kind of like my whole thing growing up—how I was raised. Try to find the positive in everything.

I was really proud of myself on that 2008 journey. I got humbled very, very quickly, professionally overseas after my ACL. When you gave me the opportunity to train with Team USA, I was so fired up! I also knew exactly what my role would be the day I stepped foot into the national team gym. You were pretty clear about the job description.

And that I think is one of the biggest things a player needs to know is what their role is going to be. For me, I was thinking, *I've got to be all-in regardless of the role, because this might be my last chance*. I didn't even know if I was going to play volleyball again after my ACL tear, so getting to the national team was a huge thing for me. I just said, "Hey, I'll work as hard as I can, I'll have to have a great attitude and help the team however I can." Embracing that role of fourth outside hitter gave me even more power to be able to influence the team in a good way, to be super positive, and find ways to help the guys who were playing.

Did it ever feel disingenuous, Scott? To me, it always looked like it was absolutely you—it was authentic.

ST: No, it was just how I felt, it was just me. I was so happy and proud to be on the team and I was in a position to do something to help, in addition to my role on the court.

You came in with such a powerful attitude. It was a refreshing approach, and it was contagious. Suddenly, people were worried less about getting theirs and were more focused on getting ours. That was huge.

ST: I was a big goal-setter back in the day. I thought, if I get a chance to play on the national team, what are my goals for this thing? The goal was always to be the best teammate. I read a lot after I tore my ACL. One of the books I read was by Vince Lombardi—I actually read it twice—about what it takes to be the best. It refers to what makes a good teammate. I said to myself, *If I get back from this ACL injury, I'm going to be the best teammate possible because that's what makes winning teams—that's what it takes to be No. 1.* It's a matter of, who's going to outwork everybody else? And who's going to be that great teammate? And so, when I got onto the team, I knew a lot of the guys, and that really helped me to live that goal because there was connection and respect already.

I felt I had to earn my spot every single day on that team. And it's that positivity that kept me going, especially on the tough days. Everybody's a pro, a former D-1 college athlete, they're all Players of the Year, they're all first-team All-Americans. I mean, you can get beat down at that level real fast. And so, it's always, okay, what's one thing I can always bring? And that's positivity. Not everyone will be receptive every day, but ultimately, it can help us get through to the next day. I would always ask myself after every practice, "Did you work hard and have you been a good teammate?"

I knew I could work harder than anybody else and still never get noticed. But working hard and being a great teammate felt [like] the only way I was going to make it onto the Olympic roster. I had nothing to lose and everything to gain.

You added value every step of the way.

ST: The guys on the team helped me too, they improved my work ethic, so I'd keep up the hope I could make it—it worked both ways. Riley [Salmon] would push me all the time, and he would always talk to me in the car when I'd be driving up to Anaheim with him and Tom [Hoff]: "Hey dude, you gotta work harder. You gotta pass more balls," or, "I need you to serve me 100 balls today and I'll serve to you." And I can remember this like it was yester-day. On the off days at the Olympics, when the main guys weren't practicing much because of the rest day in between matches, you always talked to us about how important it was to stay physically and mentally engaged, so when it's our turn to go, we're ready. And the guys who didn't play as much would train hard, and you guys coached us up. We still got after it. It was awesome, and it showed you guys, and the starters and ourselves, that we were ready when you needed us.

It's not like the people on the floor are the only ones on the team. The people who are not on the floor, the people on the bench, can make a huge difference for the entire team. They should always be supporting and pushing the team. I couldn't have picked a better group to have gone to the Olympics with. I felt like we did it the right way. The fact that we won it was kind of this cherry on top of the sundae.

Tell me about being a teammate at the Olympics. You got on the court some, not a lot, but how did you feel about that, putting so much effort into the whole process?

ST: I played every match that you put me in as well as I could. I didn't get in the gold-medal match. And that's actually the funniest thing, because people always ask me, "Aren't you upset the other guys played the gold-medal match?" The honest answer: no. The coaching staff knew where I should be and when I should be there. We rolled along the way we were supposed to. I didn't play in that match, but I know I helped us win it.

Anything else you'd like to add?

ST: There are so many variables in volleyball. It's one of the most imperfect sports I think I've ever met in my whole entire life. But a lot of it has to do with what you can control: your attitude, your communication, your effort. And if you can bring that every single day into the gym and, yeah, you know that you're going to make mistakes on the court, but you can always succeed as a teammate.

TRUST IN COACHES

Young athletes are told to do whatever the coach says. I understand the idea behind this—most youth sports are chaotic, more akin to herding kittens than anything else. Clear direction and instruction are needed. However, that blind faith—the trust that's given and not earned—can be violated, especially when the young athlete is expected to comply, no matter what. Being forced to obey, while being betrayed or abused by someone you're supposed to respect, maybe even revere, creates a lot of issues for the young athlete. Those issues, if unresolved, will fester and can negatively influence coach-athlete relationships later in life as well. I have coached athletes who have been so beaten up emotionally, so scarred and scared, that it takes months or even years for them to feel safe in the gym. The athlete's development during the time to heal, reengage, and trust again, is compromised.

Developing coach-athlete trust is about consistency of action, interaction, and intention. Are you trustworthy? I don't know, only you do, but to be an effective coach, the answer has to be yes. Creating trust is also connected to your motives, your character, your genuine care and concern for the people you coach (because they're not just "athletes"), and your relevant knowledge and information in your sport. Sport-specific knowledge aside, the great thing about the principle-based methods described in this book is that they are self-evident—they work. And it's easier for athletes to trust methods—and the coaches who use them—that are based in scientific rigor.

Interview with Lloy Ball

Lloy Ball was a member of the USA national volleyball team for 15 years—from 1993 to 2008—and participated in four Olympic Games (Atlanta 1996, Sydney 2000, Athens 2004, and Beijing 2008).

———————

Trust was a big part of our working relationship.

Lloy Ball: Yeah, it was. When I first started playing volleyball, my first real coach was my dad. Pretty tough to compare any coach after that. As far as putting the level of trust into any other person that I had with my dad, I didn't think that would ever happen. How can you put as much trust in anyone as the guy who changed your diapers and took you to little league? And to be honest, it probably set me on a path where I became a little mistrusting of other coaches after that. I knew when he was yelling at me, it was not just because he wanted me to be a better volleyball player, but because he also cared about me. Loved me. He was very good at differentiating the two roles of coach and dad as I moved through the ranks, though.

As I did move up to and into the national team program, I met other great coaches, but I never really put my trust in them. I'm sure it was my fault. As a player, I didn't accept them fully and never really put my trust in them. The maturation process is super important in sports, and it's often hard. For me, finally learning to trust a coach after my dad was part of that process.

Tell me about when we decided to bring you back to the team. [With three Olympics on his résumé, Lloy had left the team after USA finished fourth in the 2004 games.]

LB: There were some things obviously left on the table in Athens, but I would have been okay with my national team career stopping at that point. I had a wife and two small kids, and I was 35 years old. But when you asked me to come back, I knew it was the right choice for two reasons. One, I was playing the best volleyball of my career and I probably had the highest level of confidence in my own abilities. Two, you did something no one else had done or would have done: you came to a small town in the middle of a foreign country to have a cup of coffee with me and talk about playing for Team USA and the possibilities that might hold.

Talk about building trust! You showed up to spend time with me, see me play, and talk about opportunities. You made a case for how I could help you and the team get the job done. It was an important step in that ladder of trust that we climbed together. You flew thousands of miles to have a cup of coffee with me. It was the right thing to do. To share that vision for going forward and show how much you cared.

When you rejoined the team, you were the oldest guy coming into a diverse group. You had history with some of them, so there could have been some challenges when it came to reintegrating and trying to get to the Olympics and medal.

LB: You got a bunch of late twenties, mid-thirties guys who are starting second phases of their lives—married, kids, trying to put food on the table in a business that isn't easy. I was coming in for a fourth shot at the Olympics, but we had some two- and three-timers who also had not won a medal. To say there was some emotional baggage would be an understatement. But this time it felt different. Sometimes in the past were trying to over-control situations, trying to navigate a certain path toward a certain outcome. This time, you allowed us to be us. You didn't try to make any of us into someone or something else. Instead of an outcome, you moved each of us to be the best version of ourselves.

You put us in some kind of continuity, or continuous growth, so the group could function at a high level. You instilled trust in us that, if we needed to air an issue or attack a problem, you created the space for that to happen. You allowed us to be adults; we could voice our opinions, and you emphasized how to use our best qualities, instead of imposing an idea of what our best qualities were. It wasn't a matter of, "Let's plug him in here and mold him into what we think we need"—that forced leadership that tries to shove a square peg into a round hole. You wanted us to grow from the inside out.

A big shift for you was not being captain. How did that affect you and, ultimately, affect the team?

LB: I was always made the captain, and so for 10 years, at every press conference, I'd have to field questions like, "Why did you lose to that team?" While I consider myself a strong individual, after 10 years of leading a national team with average to below-average performances, to be honest, those questions got tiresome, they got heavy, and who knows how much they affected me when I got my hands on the ball?

It was actually a relief to have another veteran on the team who could take that responsibility. To be honest, being captain probably hindered me from playing my best volleyball and helping the team. The fact that you trusted me enough to not freak out when I wasn't captain anymore, but just to go and set some balls and be a kind of emotional catalyst at times, helped me and the team.

I think it helped us a ton. Just because you weren't the captain didn't mean you weren't a leader, that's for sure. We got the best of you and you were still a leader, but it was authentic. It felt like a win-win.

LB: My four Olympics were all really different—and I'm not just talking about results. In the beginning, I think most of us grew up with this notion that a team needs to be friends in order to be successful. We were afraid at times to say the things that needed to be said because of friendship. And then we had an exceptional team physically, but we didn't really care for each other. And it was hard, in a different way, in those combative moments. Ultimately, in 2008, we had a perfect balance of friends-*ish*, yet we were competitive and adult enough to challenge each other when we needed to be challenged.

When I came back in 2007, I felt like it was the first time in my tenure where there weren't 12 agendas trying to work together to win something. There was one. And obviously it's something that you helped instill. We all bought into that and told each other, "Hey, we're gonna trust this guy, this staff, because we feel like he can get us this one thing we've talked about." In the past, we let other things distract us. Not this time.

8

Mentoring

I've been coaching for a while now, and I've always been a strong advocate for developing relationships of trust with the people I coach, but I didn't really see these relationships for what they were—mentoring—until recently. The coronavirus pandemic has brought with it many challenges, one of which was a significant shift in our day-to-day with sickness, testing, isolation, and loss. There was also a significant shift in our social dynamics that led to some significant mental shifts as well. My staff and I met with our athletes weekly during the worst of the pandemic, mainly just to check in a chat, but it became clear to me over that time that these coach-athlete relationships are actually mentor-mentee relationships.

Mentoring is broadly defined as a trust-based relationship that provides psychological support and the transfer of relevant knowledge and information. Mentors can be incredibly impactful, and I'm sure we can all remember a coach or a teacher who had a profound positive influence on us. Mentoring is helping the mentee. It's a selfless investment in them; it's not about you. We've said that the holistic approach to athlete development is important, and mentoring is a critical part of that process.

Traditional mentoring is one-on-one, mentor to mentee, but mentoring can also occur between a mentor and a group of mentees. For coaches and athletes in individual sports, traditional mentoring is fine. For coaches and athletes in team sports, I think you need both. You should connect with your athletes individually and/or collectively because these relationships not only offer support and knowledge, they also provide an opportunity to build empathy and trust.

The days of hierarchical coaching (I say, "Jump." You say, "How high?") are waning. Dictatorial coaching methods lack the authentic connections required to get the work done. We can't have the inmates running the asylum, either. The coach needs to lead with a guiding hand in a velvet glove, not an iron fist, and the genuine care and concern created through the mentoring process allows that to happen.

Most younger athletes are used to hierarchical systems of coaching. The head coach is the grand poobah who sits in judgment of all things as the ultimate decision-maker. They become used to having that power wielded over them. Consequently, it takes time for these mentor-mentee relationships to develop. It takes time to build trust, but effective and efficient mentoring methods help that process. We use guiding principles to drive improvement in our skills because they work. Similarly, we should have guiding principles to drive improvement in our mentoring.

Being an effective mentor starts with authentic connection based in empathy and understanding. You have to take time to get to know your athletes, and for them to get to know you a little as well. I say "a little," because you are not there to become the athlete's friend; you are their coach, and your job is to help this person become the best they can be. Empathy and understanding will help you to do that. Shared vulnerability provides an opportunity to gain valuable insight relative to your athlete's hopes, fears, history, and operating system.

For that authentic connection to evolve, you need trust, and another way that trust is developed is through safety. These conversations become safe when the athlete knows the discussions are confidential and they can share without fear of judgment or betrayal. Also, relative to building authentic connection, make sure you are listening to understand, not just listening to reply. Trying to "win" the mentor-mentee conversation won't help you build trust.

Another way to make the space "safe" is for the coach to shift the power differential from the hierarchical coach-player to mentor-mentee—establishing a more human connection. Also, the coach has to be brave enough to admit if they don't know how to help the athlete, but also make sure they will find a person or service that can. You don't have to have all the answers, but if questions or concerns do arise, you need to help your athlete find the appropriate solutions.

In mentor meetings, I think it's more important to focus on developing the person than the athlete. Help them develop character or acquire tools and coping mechanisms to deal with the human condition, as opposed to talking about tactics or skills. Developing character off the field of play will lead to character on the field of play. It's also important to be supportive and positive in these sessions. Don't fake it, though. You can fool a fool, but you can't kid a kid. Be honest, but understand there's a need for genuine and honest optimism, belief, and positivity.

In team sports, individual mentor sessions and group mentor sessions should be guided by the responsibility you have to the team. That is to say, you're trying to help everyone, but the athletes have to understand and accept that the mentor-mentee relationship does not supersede the coach-player relationship. The coach can't start making decisions that are in the best interest of only one athlete because their ultimate responsibility—their duty, in fact—is to do what's right for the team.

In terms of frequency of meetings, let the mentee guide that process. Once a week or every couple of weeks is fine. If people are progressing nicely, once a month works too. However, meet with intent; don't meet just to meet. If there's nothing to discuss, you can have a quick chat to see how people are doing and get out of there. You can also cancel the meeting.

External factors can influence meeting frequency as well—for example, a pandemic. Also, you are a coach, not a counselor or therapist, if issues arise within your meetings that require specialist care or attention, then refer the athlete to someone with expertise in that area. Stay in your lane. You cannot, and should not, try to be all things to all people.

Educational researcher Benjamin Bloom also spoke to the importance of mentoring in learning and expertise. His 1985 study on initial and final ability also found that the influence of, and authentic connection with, the teacher or coach was a critical factor in the subject's development:

> Over and over the [young people] made reference to the impact of teachers for whom they felt love, admiration, and respect, and from whom they felt dedication to [their particular field] and to their student's development. Several said they felt they were "going nowhere" when they worked with teachers who lacked such qualities.[33]

Building theses strong mentor-mentee connections is important relative to development and achievement. A healthy mentor-mentee relationship affords the coach authentic influence, and that makes all of the changes and synergies required for significant achievement possible.

Coaches need to mentor their athletes, but I believe that they should also consider mentoring other coaches as well. As we've said, there is not a strong academic path in coaching, so coaches sharing their knowledge could help improve the quality of coaching for everyone. Most coaches are very tight-lipped, though. They don't share information for fear of losing a competitive advantage or, worse, seeming insufficient. Consequently, coaching can become an island, devoid of any real opportunities for professional development. Our university professors get to take sabbaticals, as do people in the corporate world, but coaches are not afforded any such opportunity.

I think we should reconsider the traditional "coaching island" approach. Knowing is not doing. We should not be afraid to share information, because it's the application of that information that will ultimately be the key, and if we share something and someone applies it more effectively than we do, we will learn about that improved application next time. Coaching, like competing, doesn't have to be a zero-sum endeavor. Instead of protecting our piece of the pie, coaches should consider making the pie bigger.

The New Zealand Rugby union has a different way of approaching coach development. First, they see developing the coach as a win-win, because the developing coach will then, in turn, develop the athlete. Second, mentoring is an integral part of the coaching culture of New Zealand rugby. Either formally or informally mentoring occurs on a regular basis. In line with Bloom's findings, the *who* seems to be more important that the *what*. That is, the alignment of personalities creates more positive synergy than the information itself, so choosing the right mentor is important. The purpose of these coach/mentors is to be a sounding board for ideas, challenge current thinking, and help the coach be efficient and effective in their job. It's about pushing more than pleasing or placating, though. The goal is to grow and evolve, and to that end, the mentors don't shy away from uncomfortable conversations. Operating in truth—kind, empathetic truth—is the key. Mentors are not just cheerleaders; they are an integral part of the coach's process of improvement.

In addition to this strong tradition of coach mentoring, New Zealand Rugby also hosts an annual coaching conference for coaches from the three main levels of major rugby competition in the country—the National Provincial Championship (NPC); Super Rugby; and the national team, the All Blacks. As they prepare for the conference, they contact the coaches from these respective leagues and ask them for topics. For example, what are the two things you'd like to learn more about? And who, in your opinion, is really good in those areas?

When the coaches meet, there are formal and informal discussions. The All Blacks coaches might informally discuss the latest trends they are seeing in the international arena, for instance. Then there are the formal presentations—prepared sessions given by coaches, discussing selected topics suggested by the other coaches within the NPC, Super Rugby, or All Blacks. These are coaches who often coach against each other. They are competitors, not just for outcomes on the weekends, but for other coaching jobs within the rugby world as well. It's awesome that they so openly share thoughts and ideas on topics such as skill acquisition, game tactics, strength and conditioning, and high performance. They keep open minds and share in a safe space, understanding that knowledge is one thing, but its application is another. If you only stay on your island, you'll never learn about other locations. You'll only know what you know, instead of learning what you don't know.

9

Competitive Excellence

I see competitive excellence manifested in a couple of different ways: first, and most obviously, in the actual moment of competition; and second, in the planning and preparation that goes into that moment.

COMPETITION

If you play sports, you have to learn how to compete. Someone will win and someone will lose, and that's the nature of what we sign up for. Both the moment of competition and your practices are great places to learn how to compete. The moment of competition is where the practice, planning, and preparation get put to the test. You've hopefully worked hard and worked smart to prepare; the proverbial hay is in the barn. But what does it really mean to compete? Well, to start, you don't need to live the popular narrative of having an older brother who beat up on you, never let you win, and therefore made you "tough" and competitive. The ability to compete can be expressed many different ways, and it can be learned without a bullying brother.

I think that competing well is doing your job consistently in the heat of the contest. Freeing yourself of the last play and not dwelling on the possible outcomes of the next one. Being present, being here in the now, and being able to execute. It might be acting with intelligence or courage. It might be something said, or something done. Most importantly, though, if you can be at your best when your best is needed, you're competing. Do you need to yell? Chest bump? Talk trash? Well, that's your call. But the external behaviors that are often seen as synonymous with competing could also be seen as just being loud and obnoxious. What you say is of little or no consequence, what really matters is what you *do*.

In 2018, I was invited to spend a few days with the coaches of the All Blacks. Since 1903, the All Blacks have won over 77 percent of their matches. That's the highest winning percentage of any country in world rugby. I got to know their staff and, in particular, their head coach at the time, Steve Hansen. During Steve's tenure as head coach, from 2012 to 2019, the team's winning percentage was over 89 percent. They were dominant. We talked about a lot of things, but at one point I asked him what he thought the difference was between his most successful campaigns and the ones where the team came up short. He said that the teams that succeeded were hungry, that there was a drive in them, and almost a fear that they might not succeed. As we discussed it more, neither of us liked the word *fear* or thought it was an element you wanted in your coaching or your teams, and we stumbled upon the word *edge*. That resonated. The athletes in these successful campaigns had an edge to them—a hunger to succeed and an edge. The thing I love about the word is the double entendre: they are training and competing to the edge of their skills and abilities, and they are edgy.

How did that edge get created? It turned out that his experiences were similar to mine, in that previous failures had driven future successes. Teams that had come up short carried that pain with them, and their planning, preparation, execution, and attention to detail was different the next chance they had to compete. This concept might even be corollary to the +4 percent for Csikszentmihalyi's optimal flow. Earlier in the book, I said that "winning can mask a lot of problems," and it can, but it can also create complacency. Not a complacency born of indifference, a complacency born from a lack of experience. If you've never lost, you know conceptually that the margins between winning and losing are thin, but you don't understand how thin they really are, because you've never experienced the heartache and the learning that goes with losing.

I'm not saying that you should lose to win, but I am saying that at some point it has to become personal. If you want to be the best you can be at what you do, with the hope of achieving something significant, you need the edge. You need a reason to do the work, the learning, the competing—and you need a reason to invest your life in this endeavor above all the other endeavors life has to offer. We have talked about the real costs and opportunity costs of sports, and this is another example. Without the edge, without your head and your heart, it'll be tough to make it.

Competition has been criticized by some as a negative force in our society. Alfie Kohn's *No Contest: The Case Against Competition* suggests that all competition is inherently bad for us because, at its core, it is connected to the assumption that one party can only benefit from competition at the expense of another.[34] He also states that competition undermines people's performance and productivity by creating stress and shifting our attention from doing our best to beating our opponent. It also can create hostile and/or prejudicial feelings toward, and false assumptions about, our opponent. He also asserts that competition can create negative psychological consequences for participants because it can undermine feelings of self-worth by creating fears and insecurities, reducing self-esteem, increasing anxiety and envy (especially in our world of comparison), and leading to feelings of humiliation and shame.

In contrast, David Shields and Brenda Bredemeier counter this line of thinking in their book, *True Competition*.[35] The word *competition* is derived from the Latin *petere*, meaning "to strive or to seek," combined with the prefix *com*, meaning "with." So the root meaning of competition is "to strive or seek with." The contest or event is an opportunity to strive toward or seek excellence with your opponent, trying to meet and overcome the challenge presented by each other's best efforts.

It's the outcome, though, the whole win/loss deal, that complicates things. Many people are less satisfied with best effort and best process and focus increasingly on the outcome, which leads to what Shields and Bredemeier call *decompetition*. This is the opposite of true competition, whereby the contest goals shift from doing your best against a like-minded opponent to winning at all costs at the expense of your opponent. Lying, cheating, and stealing are not competing. Anger, fighting, belittling, or demeaning are not competing, either. The moral compass shifts, and people are now engaged in a fundamentally different pursuit, namely their own success at another's expense. It becomes binary, a zero-sum game. They are engaged in the contest, but they are not truly competing. So, while competition and decompetition look alike, in terms of the structure of the contest, the values driving each are different, as are the consequences.

Sheilds and Bredemeier suggest that the majority of findings that Kohn references in his book are actually examples of decompetition, which is our natural default and is not healthy or positive for our society. But, as always, we have a choice, and actively choosing true competition can be incredibly positive. It leads to the pursuit of excellence and the profound enjoyment and satisfaction that goes with it.

When I came to the United States, I had to learn how to compete. I didn't really know what true competition looked like growing up. Neither of my parents played competitive sports, and New Zealand culture, at that time, seemed much more collaborative than competitive. Also New Zealand's popular narrative around achievement was grounded in "tall poppy" syndrome, the phenomenon where the high achieving or successful "tall poppy" gets cut down to size. The lesson being that you should never stick out above your peers. So, through that lens, my perception of competition was closer to decompetition than true competition.

During my time as an athlete and a coach here in America, I have learned, and can attest to, the powerful positive benefits of competition. I agree with Shields and Bredemeier that true competition is a net positive for our society because it teaches us how to pursue excellence. Teaching our athletes how to compete makes them better at competing. They become more resilient, more capable, and more engaged. Competition is a tough teacher, but it's honest and true. I also agree with Kohn— though I would suggest he consider the term *decompetition* to describe his analysis—because the negative consequences he describes are a direct product of that connotation.

We need to teach our athletes to compete, understanding that they will experience both competition and decompetition during the contest. But, as always, when decompetition creeps in, they have a choice. They can respond to the response and keep decompetition at bay.

PLANNING AND PREPARATION

To me, planning and preparation are about trying to manage as many of the variables specific to your sport, the level of competition, the age of your athletes, and so on as you can. There's power in the details. Regardless of your level, how you plan and prepare to compete will influence how you compete. The process of competitive excellence is challenging, especially for the athletes. To that end, I want them to focus their effort and energy on working, learning, and competing. If we can make that process a little bit, or a lot, easier for them through our planning and preparation, then we should.

We can define planning as the process of designing a framework of intended action. We've discussed game plans and practice plans, but there should be plans for things like your athletes' physical training and recovery as well. Plans should be detailed and comprehensive. For example, you can create a sleep plan to help you with nighttime sleep, napping, managing jetlag, and adjusting circadian rhythms through light exposure. Plans also need to be flexible—that is, circumstances around the competitive environment might change, and we have to be able to compensate and adjust when those changes occur. Travel, accommodation, nutrition, hydration, visualization, you name it—you can plan it. Planning gives structure and routine to your process. It can also build trust.

We can define preparation as the process of getting ready for a future event. Planning will be an important part of our preparation. For our athlete, preparing could be connected to considerations leading up to the moment of competition, for example, packing their bags to travel, or making sure they get plenty of sleep. Or their preparation might be connected to the moment of competition itself, for example, reviewing a game plan, or executing an in-contest performance routine.

As Benjamin Franklin said, "Failing to prepare is preparing to fail," and, given that the moment of competition presents plenty of elements that are beyond our control, it becomes imperative that we plan and prepare to control the things that we can.

Interview with Rich Lambourne

Rich Lambourne joined the U.S. men's national team in 2000 as a libero, a position that specializes primarily in serve receive and back-row defense. Rich was an alternate for the 2004 Games and made his Olympic debut at the 2008 Olympics, helping Team USA win gold.

Based on your experience with Team USA, how would you describe the team's commitment to competitive excellence?

Rich Lambourne: Well, we competed a lot—in practice and in matches. We got pretty good at it. One of the cool things about that group was the commitment to adding something every day, trying to get a little bit better. You kept that process going by giving us little cues, technical stuff or base position or something. We weren't bombarded with information, but I felt like we got a lot of it. We got better most days.

Better at what?

RL: All of it, I guess—skills and how to execute them, the whole process-versus-results kind of stuff. Certainly, I was never aware of that language until you were coaching us. And that was a big hallmark of our team, this process we were committed to. Obviously, we played plenty of matches, and we cared about the result, but there was this whole process that we were going through in training, trying to acquire skills or maybe skill level, that reinforced our confidence in the mission and our team. That seemed to be the focus.

You were there for all of it. From the first practice in 2005 to the last match in Beijing. You saw how it evolved, how the team improved. Obviously, it wasn't easy, but we tried to get better every day and apply what we learned in the moment of competition. Any thoughts about that?

RL: There weren't many bad practices. Guys were bringing it pretty consistently. And you did specific things to help us work together, with the mission and stuff. That affected how we practiced and the whole competitive excellence thing. To get the success we did in 2008 meant we had to figure out a lot of stuff in the years leading up to it. There were plenty of bumps in the road, we had to make a lot of changes.

Tell me more about that.

RL: I probably had a different perspective on it all than some of the others. I'd worked with you at BYU, and then you were our assistant coach for three years before taking over the head coaching role. My level of confidence with you was solid. But when you took over as the coach in 2005, and we were sitting in a conference room putting together a mission statement and your only demand was to start with, "We will win a gold medal in Beijing," everyone, myself included, found that pretty laughable because we hadn't really done squat.

We had a good 2005, but the wheels started coming off the bus a little bit in 2006. My faith in your process wasn't wavering, but that for sure was not the case for some of my teammates. We got through it, though. We got back to work and stayed the course. We owned it and learned from it. You have to get real with people or nothing's ever going to change. It's much easier to operate in a space where everyone's telling you you're good and that it's not your fault. You know? You think you're good and no one's saying what you really need to hear: "Here are the gaps in your game." No one wants to hear that, but that's what we had to do to build a competitive team—find the weaknesses and become a team with authentic connection on the court.

What stands out to me—what instigated the shift we needed—is your consistency in adherence to the path that we'd laid out in that meeting on mission. You also had the strength to stand up to some pretty large personalities on that team and that conviction in what you knew to be the correct path got the buy-in we needed as a team. And that was critical to our success.

What were things that made the biggest difference in practice?

RL: Working smart, not long. Quality over quantity. It wasn't like, "Hey, we've got three hours blocked off for today, so we're going to go hard for 180 minutes. I got my stopwatch here." It was, "Here are these six drills I have for today. If by drill four, we're humming at a good pace and we're all crushing it, we're going to leave on a high note." Knowing we'd get rewarded for maximum effort no matter how long we practiced definitely put the emphasis on quality over quantity.

There was also this notion we shared of training being just as difficult as matches, if not more so. Our guys would go up against each other, battling every day. It was intense. And we were always pretty evenly matched, so it was always competitive.

It was also a lot of fun to go all out like that and get the competitive juices flowing. Then we'd go into matches with a decent level of confidence. When we were playing the top teams—Brazil, Russia, and so forth—there's the nerves that come along with playing meaningful matches, but toward the end of the quad, it always felt like we were in control. Another benefit of the way we trained was that our skills and our attitudes helped us nearly always beat the teams that we should beat. We were consistent.

In fact, I've had people tell me that, if you just looked at our faces or the way we were competing, you wouldn't know the score. You wouldn't know if we were up or down. I thought that was a pretty cool compliment.

We also developed good synergy, we learned how to play together, and we worked hard to get that over the four years. We had to kill a lot of demons on and off the court, but we made it, we stayed on the path you had in mind for us, and we won. We did what we set out to do.

What about the planning and preparation? Any thought on that?

RL: I didn't see too much of that. It felt like you were almost trying to shield us from it, so we could just focus on competing. It seemed like you guys had everything under control. The game plans were solid, practice was always planned, the travel was pretty seamless. We felt prepared. It felt like we didn't leave too much to chance.

10

Culture

Another challenge, in our process of excellence, is building a culture that supports the kind of effort and commitment required for significant achievement. Culture represents the behaviors and norms of a group of people. It encompasses knowledge, beliefs, and identity, but culture is more than the dictionary meanings of these words, it's the way the words are lived. Ideally, when the culture is strong, the space between what you say and subsequent actions that support those words is very small.

When discussing culture with groups, I suggest the following litmus test to assess its strength. You and someone else in your team or organization should separately write down what you both think the cultural foundations of your group are. Describe them as best you can. What are the fundamental tenets, and how are those tenets lived or expressed? Now compare notes. If you both describe the culture and the supporting behaviors in a similar way, then I would suggest that your culture is clearly defined and strong. If the descriptions are different, then perhaps you have an opportunity for improvement. Lastly, if you're the leader of this endeavor, know that everyone will be watching you. You must live the goal and the mission better than anyone.

If culture beats strategy, then what's best is having strength in both. I have found that the goal and the supporting behaviors have a big impact on the culture of teams. Identifying the outcome and formulating a principle-based pathway to its achievement that is authentic to the group, is critical. The importance of this connection, between the goal and the group, is why we want all the stakeholders to have a voice in the goal-setting process. This connection, between the outcome goal and the people who are working to achieve it, also promotes buy-in, creates team identity, and strengthens belief.

Any team involves multiple personal agendas, and it's unlikely you can satisfy all of them. One person wants a lot of playing time; another wants to score a record number of points; another wants to win a championship. Yet a major contributor to team excellence is getting everyone to support the team agenda and the team goal. There is a requirement for the selfless pursuit of team mastery: the individual players need to support the team agenda ahead of their own. These agendas don't need to be mutually exclusive, but the priority of "ours before yours" must be clear. For example, committing to the pursuit of competitive excellence rather than fixating on winning the championship or receiving an individual accolade, yields a better chance of being part of a championship team and, as a result of that commitment and the team's success, earning the coveted award. Don't let what you want get in the way of what you have to do to get it. It's also worth noting that if you are on a gold-medal team, even if you didn't play much, you are still an Olympic gold medalist. No one asks you how many points you scored or how much playing time you got; they just want to see your medal!

The question then becomes, Who does get to be on the team? Who earns the opportunity to pursue significant achievement?

As the coach, you'll need some athletes and you'll need people to help you. But how do you select a team? And how do you recruit your staff?

Roster selection is important. You should start by selecting the best athletes/players. You can't win the derby on a donkey, you'll need some thoroughbreds, and as it turns out, the better the athletes you recruit to your teams, the better coach you become. In all seriousness, though, the people you select matter.

The day you announce the Olympic team is a tough one for the athletes. Some coaches might try to convince you that it's a tough day for them, but they still get to come to work the next day and didn't have their life's dream crushed the day before. There are 12 indoor volleyball athletes that get to represent their country at the Olympics, and for those 12, the day you become an Olympian, or are selected to repeat as one, is a day to savor.

The first eight or nine roster spots should be your best, most talented players by position. The next three or four selections are more challenging. I have found, through experience, that selecting the 12 best players can be a mistake. An all-star team can bring with it all-star egos, and you tend to get more competition within the group than collaboration. Once you have selected your eight or nine, then it's time to select to role and to character. For example, the second-best volleyball setter (by skill) might not be the best second setter (by role). In other words, you need athletes who can not only perform at a very high level, they also have to be able to support the team and the athletes ahead of them. These are athletes who might not get to compete and yet still say and do everything they can to help the team. That balance of skill, ego, selflessness, and authentic value-add connection is critical. It's four years to be good for two weeks to hope to be great for the last two hours. You need people who are committed to the team, even if they're not getting their personal Olympic hopes and dreams realized.

Selecting to role is as critical to a team's success as selecting to ability, and connected to that concept is role clarity. Make sure everyone is clear on what their responsibility is and how that connects and adds value to achieving the outcome goal. The athletes need to feel connected to the mission, even if it's not in the way they might have envisioned. Communicating that expectation and validating it, catching them being a great teammate, not just a great athlete, helps to reinforce their role and their importance to the team. Some of the most important people on your team will not play a significant role on the field of play, but they can have a profound influence on what happens out there. There are lots of ways to say and do everything you can to help your team win.

Another mechanism to facilitate role clarity and role acceptance is using the word *today*. Make sure your athletes hear and understand that this is their role today. Through their efforts, an injury, a tactical adjustment, or any number of other reasons, that role might be different tomorrow—and they need to be ready. Telling your athletes "this is your role *period*" sounds like you've made concrete, irreversible decisions. "This is your role today" is not only accurate, it allows the athlete to feel more connected to the team and the goal.

Even with role clarity and commitment, you'll still have problems. Everyone has baggage; it's just that some people's suitcases are bigger than others, and we all struggle from time to time. Occasional bad behavior is one thing, but dysfunction is something you have to address, and I do have a concept to help manage it—the Rule of 1.5. You need to protect your athletes and culture, and to that end you should have no more than one-and-a-half people who are not culturally aligned on your team at any given time. The "one" has to be extremely talented, and the "half" could be me today, it might be you tomorrow, because we'll all have an off day at some point. However, once you have two people who aren't supporting the team's agenda, you will have a clique, and they'll start recruiting others to strengthen and validate their behavior. Then you're in trouble. The first rule of behavior is that you get what you tolerate. So, if someone is exceptionally gifted and the value-add of their talent and skill outweighs the negatives, you have to consider keeping them around. However, I think you should only tolerate dysfunction until you can either teach that person to become functional, or until you can replace them.

You also have to hire or select a staff to help you. You should surround yourself with the best people you can. In addition to relevant knowledge and experience, there are three main things I look for when hiring. First is a significant capacity for work; they have to be able to grind. Second, I need a certain type of loyalty. Not the blind kind, but the type of loyalty that may privately disagree with something we're doing behind closed doors, but will publicly support it once a decision is made. Third, I need principle alignment; we should agree on our guiding principles. We can disagree about how the principles are applied, but if we disagree about the fact that we live on planet Earth and laws of physics apply, then we probably won't work well together. I don't need agreement, because if we're all thinking alike, no one is thinking very much, but alignment is key.

Most often, when we're recruiting and selecting people to join our programs, we look at historical individual performance as the main evaluative criterion for selection. If we're not getting the caliber of talent that our competitors are, or even if we are, I think recruiting to potential is equally as important as recruiting to performance. Does this person have the ability to learn and make change? Do they play well with others? Can we see who they can become in our program versus who they have been in someone else's? And, knowing that a better you makes a better us, are they the type of low-ego, high-output person who is prepared to put the team agenda ahead of their own? Will they work hard to be the best they can be and help others to that same end as well?

You not only need to align with the people you hire, but you also need to align with the people who hired you. I ask my direct reports this question: Would you prefer that I work for you or that I work with you? The answer helps frame how the working relationship goes moving forward. If I'm working for you, it's a more vertically integrated organizational structure, and at least for me, it feels a little more constrained relative to the type of communication it affords. It also creates some boundaries in terms of the professional relationship. That doesn't mean it's bad, but it's good to know going in. If they want to work with you, then you have the opportunity to connect with them in a more authentic way. As they work with you and your program more closely, there will generally be more synergies created. There's better flow of information, more constructive conversations regarding strategy and deployment of resources, and better problem-solving.

It's also important to ask your direct reports what their outcome expectations are for the program you're coaching. If they are thinking you need to win the national championship every year, and you're thinking you'll be happy if the team breaks .500, then you need to find a way to resolve that expectation gap. Also, if they're saying "national championship" but are not providing national championship resources, you have another space that needs to be discussed and resolved. You need to share with your direct report your goals and your vision for the program, and then make sure you agree that both are appropriate, relative to what's expected. Then you need to make sure you're going to be supported in a way that can allow those expectations to be realized.

I think it's important to have direct and honest communication with your staff, and to that end, I think it's important to have regular staff meetings. I have always tried to connect our program's major stakeholders through our staff meetings. I want everyone in the room—strength and conditioning coaches, sports medicine, operations and logistics, and our media person as well. The reason I want them all in there is so everyone hears what everyone else is up to, what issues or concerns they have, or the great work they're doing. It's a safe, confidential space. When everyone is "in the know," you get some great cross-pollination, you get strategic alignment, consistency of messaging across you whole group, strengthening of culture, and it builds trust.

If we keep things separate, that can lead to silos within your program, spaces in communication that will get filled with assumptions instead of facts. I think that silos can lead to agendas, and now you're not working as efficiently and effectively as you could.

Interview with Ryan Millar

Ryan Millar is a three-time indoor volleyball Olympian (2000, 2004, and 2008) and an NCAA national champion. He helped USA win gold in Beijing.

What can you tell me about the culture of that 2008 group? How did it evolve?

Ryan Millar: I'm working in the leadership/culture management space now, so I love these conversations. What I think is that people will work hardest for a cause or a purpose, I think a big part of what you were able to do during those four years, trying to win the Olympics, was you really connected us to the purpose of why we were there.

And in the past, we had never really had any conversations or communication around what our purpose truly was. It wasn't really something that was on our brains. It was just kind of like, *Well, we're good. So let's go out and play hard, and most of the time we'll win*. But that on its own isn't super engaging. You had us connect to something bigger than that, something we'd all hoped to achieve.

So would you say that this unifying theme facilitated better learning or made the teaching methods and practices more impactful? Did it make people more open to change?

RM: Yeah, I absolutely do. When you created that unification process, I think you saw an openness or willingness of the guys in the gym to recognize that, you know, we're not the best team in the world right now, we're not the strongest or the tallest. So we had to figure out what our strength could be and then work to improve. And once we had that recipe baked, it was kind of like, *Well, okay, now we can have a chance to do what we set out to do*.

So how does that culture feel? Can you describe it?

RM: Success breeds success. And so we did get a little bit of momentum early in the quad, but it was choppy at times too. I think the shift in thinking really happened as we started truly understanding that our team was good enough to produce the types of outcomes that we all felt like we could, because culture is really all about the way we think, right? It's about why we do the things that we do, and if you've got the right thinking in place among a group of guys who are battling to make the Olympic team and try and win the whole thing, then culture plays a massive part in that because the culture actually produces the types of behaviors and outcomes that you want. So it's the beliefs that you hold that drive the actions that you take.

So I felt like you did a really good job aligning our thinking around the goals in terms of the things that we needed to be doing every day at practice and in the weight room and working with our athletic trainer. It was getting our bodies right and getting our minds right in order for us to believe we could perform at the highest level on a daily basis. A lot of it was a function of how you guys worked together as a coaching staff and then how we worked together as a team, and then our ability to be open and receptive to the coaching that you guys were going to be giving us.

How about in matches?

RM: In matches we were calm. There was emotion, of course, but we were in control. We battled so much in practice that the matches were fine. When we needed to reset, like a timeout or something, you and the other coaches did a really good job of utilizing the very first part of it for us to kind of just cool down a little bit, because maybe we're in a heated battle and there's something intense going on. It was calm, we'd have a chance to take a breath, and then it was always right into the one or two things that we could immediately do that could impact the game.

And there was a lot of that communication going on during the matches between us. We were talking about the plan and talking about adjustments, helping each other out. It was more talking than yelling, you know? We'd celebrate the points, but between points we were trying to get ready for the next one. It wasn't just noise. If we got into trouble, if we were down, it stayed the same. Let's side-out, and then we'll score some points and we'll be right back in the game.

So, if you can describe that team in one word, what would it be?

RM: Oh man. I would say "ballers." When I think of that team, I just think ballers. That team just went out, and maybe this is a culture thing, but we played our style of volleyball. We weren't trying to be anyone other than ourselves. It felt authentic, you know?

Yeah, I agree. We had the right system for our team, for the athletes we had. Anything else culturally, about that group?

RM: You know, we weren't all best friends. We're still not all best friends. We have gone through this unbelievable, uncommon journey, and we're connected by that. But the big thing was this: when it was go-time, there was mutual respect and there was a ton of trust on that team that was built and created over time. And I think it got to a level of, look, personality aside, temperament aside, lifestyle choices aside, no one really cared about all of that stuff, because when we got on the court, we knew what we had to do. And we also knew that, when the time came, everyone was going to have each other's backs, no matter what, because we were all in this thing together and we were marching toward this common purpose. And that's the real value of engagement and connection, when everybody is moving in the right direction together, no matter where they're from, what their philosophies are in life, or whatever. When we get on the court, it's go-time. I think that's kind of a baller mindset.

What did you think about conflict resolution? I mean, that's an important product of culture. Did we deal with it, or did we sweep it under the carpet?

RM: I remember plenty of times when we would have arguments in the gym or issues within the team. But I thought you helped us create a really good system to manage conflict, because it happens, and we didn't shy away from it. You just tried to give us the tools to get through it and put a leadership structure in place that could help us manage it. You know what I mean? Tom [the team's captain] was phenomenal. He was great at reminding guys why we were there and that what we were trying to do was way bigger than whatever disagreement they were having. The expectation was that you deal with it directly, you know, and if there's an issue, then you and that person figure it out versus talking about it with others or just letting it fester. Figure it out and move on.

Anything else you want to add?

RM: The culture was strong, resilient. We could deal with the tough stuff, the adversity, and that speaks to the strength of it right there. It was a special group. It was a special time. It's not easy winning gold medals.

11

Mental, Physical, and Social Considerations

As you can see, the process of competitive excellence is multifaceted, and the way we approach it should be, too. We should understand all the parts to performance so we can better execute the whole performance. We have covered many of the parts of this process in detail, but there are other elements of that we need to discuss.

PHYSICAL CONSIDERATIONS

We've described, in reasonable detail, the process of acquiring and applying the physical skills required to give you the best possible chance of achieving your outcome goal. Here are some other aspects of physical preparation that you should consider in your pursuit of significant achievement.

Sleep

Sleep is essential for overall health and well-being. Everyone needs sleep in order to recover and function well the next day. In addition to being restorative, sleep affords us the opportunity for immune system and cardiovascular responses, which keep us healthy. In addition to the physical benefits of sleep, there are a number of mental benefits as well. Sleep is essential for optimal cognitive function. We've discussed performance degradation and reduced learning due to fatigue. Lack of sleep can also negatively influence other physical factors, such as reaction time, and increase the risk of injury.

Sleep-management strategies can vary depending on the individual. Educating athletes regarding the need for sleep and how to prepare themselves and their environment for optimal sleep is beneficial in a variety of ways. Empowering and preparing them to be able to plan and be accountable for their sleep responsibilities will pay dividends as they progress through their athletic careers.

When you get enough sleep, your mood improves, and that can positively influence your mental health and well-being. So it turns out, contrary to popular belief, that snoozing is not losing. Getting enough sleep actually increases your chances of winning.

Nutrition

If you're going to be an athlete, you need to fuel like one. Your ability to perform depends on physical and mental skills such as strength, endurance, and cognitive ability, and all of these are connected to the way you fuel. Athletes need vegetables, fruits, carbohydrates, fats, and proteins like the rest of us. They need good sources of nutrition that will provide enough calories to give them the energy to compete and the vitamins and minerals needed to support bodily functions.

Sports nutrition includes fueling, hydration, and recovery. Each athlete will have different needs in these areas depending on their age, height, weight, and the demands of their sport. Fueling refers to the types of foods you consume and when you consume them. The mix of carbs, fats, and proteins, and the amounts, pre- and post-training, are possible factors to consider for optimal performance. In general, though, you should look to replace the calories you burned that day.

Hydration is a huge part of optimal performance in sports, and again, depending on the demands of the sport and athlete, the required amounts and frequency will differ. The human body is made up of nearly 60 percent water, and during physical activity you will lose some of that fluid through sweat. Drinking water is the best way to rehydrate.

For shorter events (under an hour), water can replace what you lose from sweating. For longer events, you may benefit from a mix of water and sports drinks. They provide electrolytes and carbohydrates, often in the form of salt and sugar. Many of these sports drinks are tailored to taste specifications, not necessarily to nutritional ones. Consequently, there can be significant amounts of sugar in these products, so relying exclusively on sports drinks may not be an optimal hydration strategy.

Hydration should be addressed throughout the day, especially during periods of training and competition. The fluids consumed during activity often do little to hydrate the body, so it's important to adequately hydrate prior to training and competition. The general rule of thumb is that if you're thirsty, you're already dehydrated. So make sure you hydrate before the contest, otherwise you could be operating at a physiological disadvantage.

Caffeine consumption should also be considered. Like all of us, athletes have access to beverages that are highly caffeinated. Caution should be exercised when consuming these drinks around training or competition. The sugar and caffeine can cause the athlete to "crash," and they can sometimes suppress feelings of hunger, leading to insufficient fueling. In younger athletes, especially, these drinks can have less-than-optimal performance effects.

Eating to support recovery means making that sure you're using nutrition to optimize healing after you've trained or competed. Again, like fueling, post-workout nutrition depends on many factors specific to the athlete and the sport. A great example of a convenient recovery food is chocolate milk. Many nutritionists recommend it after exercise, as the protein in the milk helps with muscle recovery and the sugar can be quickly absorbed to replace muscle glycogen.

We educate our athletes about food, but we should also teach them how to buy it and how to cook it. People assume that athletes know how to do this, but many have been too busy training and competing to learn. Our nutritional education, relative to the types of foods we should eat and portion sizes, is largely theoretical; we have to make it practical.

Planning healthy, nutritious meals is important. You are what you eat, and the connection between good, healthy food and good performance is real. Learning to shop, to buy fresh fruits and vegetables that will last, reading food labels, and learning to work within a budget are all valuable skills.

We need to teach them to cook. They don't need to prepare duck à l'orange, but they have to progress past toast and instant ramen. Helping athletes learn how to find tasty recipes and then cook them properly is critical. For example, making sure vegetables are not overcooked, that they haven't had all the nutritional value cooked out of them, is a good skill to learn. The other benefit from learning how to cook is that well-cooked food tastes much better, and is consumed in larger quantities, than food that's been cooked poorly.

We also know that the time demands on our athletes are real. Preparing food and cooking meals takes time, and there are commercially packaged supplemental foods that have high-quality ingredients, appropriate nutritional value, and can make fueling a little easier for busy athletes. The use of these products should be seen as an additional fueling strategy, not a meal-replacement strategy.

Breathing

We talk a lot about breathing in this book, and we should, it's important. But how we breathe matters as well. Breathing all the way in and all the way out helps in a number of physical and mental ways. Aside from the obvious transfer of oxygen and carbon dioxide, deep breathing helps with quality of sleep, digestion, your body's immune responses, and it can reduce stress levels. It also affords mental clarity and provides that all-important space between emotion and action. Breathe deep—it gets oxygen to the body and oxygen to the brain, and you'll be better for it.

Training

We should train physically to prepare for practice and competition. Strength, endurance (muscular and cardiovascular), speed, quickness, and power are all systems that we might have to engage in our sport. Developing and increasing capacities in these areas allow us to sustain longer periods of maximum effort and performance, and facilitates better recovery.

In physical preparation and performance training, the S.A.I.D. principle refers to "specific adaptations to imposed demands." Simply put, when we place a stressor on the body, it responds by preparing itself to deal with that stressor when it's presented again. With this in mind, it's important to consider the needs of your sport, position within the sport, and individual needs (am I naturally fast/slow, and so on) when determining what activities should be included in a physical training program.

To be a successful part of athletic development, physical training programs should be done on a consistent basis, should be appropriate to the athlete's training history, and should change as the athlete grows and develops. For example, beginner-level athletes may start by mastering general athletic movement patterns, such as squatting and lunging using only bodyweight, and once they become proficient in those patterns, they can gradually add external load to those movements.

Strength training is an important quality to develop for any athlete. It is a primary component of other qualities, such as power, speed, and endurance. However, once a foundation of strength has been developed, there is a diminishing return on transfer to sports performance due to the speed at which sporting movements occur. Therefore, an athlete who has mastered foundational strength movements and possesses adequate strength levels for their sport, should really look to what qualities have the greatest impact on their sports performance and engage in a program that would reflect those as a priority.

Sports Medicine

Access to qualified sports medicine professionals is essential. Athletes get sick, they get injured, and we have to take care of them. In the event an athlete sustains an injury that doesn't require emergency care (always refer to a physician in those cases), there are effective strategies to initially manage it.

The P.R.I.C.E. principle includes protection, rest, ice, compression, and elevation. These can be used effectively for many musculoskeletal injuries. Protect the injury from further damage by splinting, bandaging, and/or modifying activity. Rest the injury for the first few days. The length of rest can vary depending on the injury location and severity. Ice for 15–20 minutes every two to three hours as a general guideline. Be aware of negative effects of ice, such as skin injury and circulation deficits. Ice should not be used over open wounds, and use caution when ice is applied to areas where nerves are close to the skin (for example, the elbow). Compression is used to assist with swelling control and movement restrictions. Elevation of the injured area should be above the level of the heart to aid circulation to the injured area and reduce swelling. Please note that these suggestions should never take the place of qualified medical advice or instruction from a trained medical professional.

Training and competing in athletics can take a physical, mental, and physiological toll on your body. Your body may not always feel great, especially during intense physical activity. Pain is a complex process that can mean different things to different individuals; however, pain is also your body's way of communicating. The ability to distinguish between pain and discomfort is not easy. Athletes should be educated and feel comfortable to express their pain and have the appropriate accommodations made for them. Education regarding the injury and healing process can help athletes learn how to differentiate pain from discomfort and better understand their capacities and limitations.

Recovery

A lot of attention has been given to athlete recovery over the past few years. Effective recovery strategies have been shown to counteract the physiological and psychological effects of sports, such as fatigue or muscle soreness. Implementation of the restorative recovery process can allow athletes to train or compete again at an appropriate level of effort, intensity, and execution. Recovery protocols can involve heat, cryotherapy (cold), soft-tissue manipulation (massage/body work techniques, foam rollers), compression devices, or a combination of any of these modalities. Sleep is also a critical part of the recovery process for athletes, as are hydration and fueling.

Athletes should have a clear understanding, through talking with a medical professional, of their recovery goals, and they should formulate a plan to accomplish them. An optimal recovery plan should take into consideration the demands of the sport as well as the athletes' own individual needs. This will help guide the athlete to the modalities or methods that will be most effective for them.

There are simple, inexpensive ways to manage an effective recovery protocol, but the athlete must understand that the protocol could change over the different phases of training and competition. Utilizing equipment that is portable and easy to use as well as finding modalities that work well, relative to the athlete's recovery goals, is a good place to start. The athlete's consistency and compliance will be the most significant factors influencing the effectiveness of their recovery program.

MENTAL CONSIDERATIONS

Competing in sports is a physical contest that demands controlled and intense mental focus, physical skill, and effort. The mental game is important, but competition is not an intellectual exercise, it's a physical exercise that can be improved through the application of mental skills. The mental game is played between the moments of physical activity.

When people think about the mental aspects of sports performance, the most common consideration is the idea of pressure, which, to paraphrase social psychologist Roy Baumeister, can be defined as an emotional response caused by factors that increase the importance of performing well in a particular moment.[36] But as I said earlier, whatever you feel about the moment, the moment doesn't feel anything about you.

Expectations are another part of the mental puzzle. Again, we assign an emotional response to something we hope will happen in the future. Or possibly even worse, something that someone else hopes for our future. In today's world, with the prevalence of social media, athletes have to learn how to manage not only their own expectations, but the expectations of others as well. Often, the others are people they don't even know. Athletes have to set boundaries as to what is their stuff, what they should attend to and try to control, and what is not their stuff, and let the stuff that's not theirs go. Family, friends, coaches, social media, or news media—it's a lot for anyone to deal with. The most important expectation is what you expect from yourself. That's the most important question to answer.

Dr. Ken Ravizza was a giant in the world of sports psychology. While most of his work was in baseball, I was able to convince him to consult with our USA men's and women's volleyball teams, and he also spent some time in our gym in Minnesota. His approach to sports psychology started with identifying and understanding the *why* of the athlete's participation in their sport. This was critical to giving direction and meaning to the *how* of achievement. The core tenet of his approach to was to control the controllables, with the extension being that if the athlete could learn to control themselves, they could learn to control their performance as well. If the athlete could learn to self-regulate in the different phases of the contest—preparation, competition, and then review (to get the lessons learned)—they would consistently be able to perform to the best of their ability.

Controlling your preparation is a significant task. Increasing your capacity in this area is a big deal. It could be goal clarity, skill acquisition, practice planning, systems, tactics, logistics, or anything that can lead to an improvement in performance. In the moment of competition itself, control is expressed by being present—competing play to play, point to point, possession to possession. Then the review, being able to make an honest subjective evaluation of your performance and interpret and evaluate the objective statistics and video as well. The athlete should try to find the things they did well and identify the main opportunities for improvement, to frame the next preparation phase.

All of this must be then evaluated through the lens of the athlete's perception. How did the athlete see or feel about themselves and their performance? What did they think about the coach, the plan, the team, and so on? Are they clear and aligned? Or are their feelings causing discord and pulling them away from the goal? If the perception does not match the reality, then we need to bring the athlete back to the present, to the reality of what happened, and back to the process of controlling the things that they can.

The athlete's ability to be present, to know where they're at is critical. They need to compete to win, but they must also understand that focusing on the process will give them a better chance of achieving that. They have to control the things they can, including themselves and own their performance. There will be days when they're not feeling great, when they're feeling tired or a little-off, but as Ken would say, "Feeling good is overrated." He would ask, "Are you that bad that you have to feel good to play good?" It's a great question. The reality of sports, and life for that matter, is that you're not going to feel good all the time, so what will you choose to do? Will you define the moment or will the moment define you? Can you give 100 percent of your B game or your C game to the moment of competition? Or will you wallow in self-pity, choose to be a victim of your feels, and disengage?

Another difference between the greats and the goods in sports is their ability to compete, to give everything they have to the moment of competition, even when it's difficult to do so. When there are plenty of reasons not to give it their all, and yet, in spite of how they feel, these athletes engage and compete and get the job done with whatever they've got. As Ravi would say, they have a good crummy day.

A particularly effective mechanism to develop this ability for athletes in team sports, aside from the obvious discipline and self-control, is to have them move their attention away from their own shortcomings and focus on helping the team. For the athlete, dwelling on the fact that they are struggling, often leads to more struggles. Instead of forcing their A game, or feeling sorry for themselves that they don't have it, they should consider helping their teammates to make up the difference for their decreased performance by doing things like talking about the plan or encouraging them, and then celebrating their successes. Give energy to the team, don't selfishly take it away because you're not performing to your expectations. Be grateful and appreciative that your teammates are getting it done for you, and help them in any way that you can. This outward focus often leads to improved performance for both the athlete who is struggling and the team.

Coaches often end up becoming the conduit to many of these mental-game strategies. They should learn about and embrace the mental game and weave it into the way they plan and execute practice and competition. Most of the time, the coach will be the one trying to help bring the athlete back to the moment. To do that, they must learn to say the right thing, at the right time, with the right tone.

Athletes are not machines. They are people and are, quite possibly, more prone to mental health issues than the rest of the population. For example, the athlete who works incredibly hard and trains relentlessly might be seen, in the real world, to possess obsessive-compulsive traits. The line between dedication and compulsion is blurred. I use this example not do diminish the incredible amount of hard work that elite athletes do but to show that they are human and they are prone to all of the frailties that go with that condition.

At the time of writing, we are still battling the coronavirus pandemic. The last couple of years have been atypical, to say the least, and our athletes (like the rest of us) were ill-equipped to deal with the isolation, testing, stress, fear, and loss that came with the virus. Any cracks in their mental health became chasms, and many needed mental and emotional support. We have been fortunate that our recent generations have not had to endure a global crisis, and consequently, when the pandemic hit, we all lacked the mental skills to manage it. Not because we were deficient, we just lacked experience, which as you'll remember is the best teacher. The pandemic has been hard, it has presented numerous challenges, but like all moments of adversity, we can learn and grow from our experience.

Our elite athletes, especially in the Olympic arena, are often encumbered by the mental and emotional burden of expectation and the subsequent pressure that comes with it. Most notably, USA Olympians Simone Biles and Mikayla Shiffren, both expected to be multiple gold-medal winners in their respective events, struggled. A recent Associated Press article sums up Shiffren's feelings about the expectations of Olympic success perfectly:

"It has to be gold or else that's a huge disappointment."

For Biles, Shiffrin realized, "It even went a step beyond that. It wouldn't have been a "disappointment"; people just didn't even consider it a possibility. And what I know from that kind of pressure is: It is not easy to win. Ever."

Wrap all of it up, she continued, and the Games themselves are "not really an enjoyable process overall."

Yes, Shiffrin acknowledged, there are wonderful snippets. Memories to cherish for a lifetime. And, yes, those make everything "worth it."

"But it's not like rainbows and sunshine and butterflies and everything that people sort of say," Shiffrin said. "They're like, 'Wow, that looks like it was so much fun!' And you're like, 'Well, it was fun to cross through the finish line and, in the next five seconds, see the green light (signaling the fastest time) and comprehend that. That was a fun thing.' And the rest of the day—the whole rest of the day—was really, really pretty stressful and uncomfortable."[37]

We all struggle, but for these unbelievable athletes and many others, their struggles were played out on a global stage, under immense scrutiny. They were reduced, dehumanized in the media, to something less because of a few mistakes that may well have been connected to the unrealistic expectations created around their performance. It was heartbreaking, disappointing, and frustrating to see how they were treated and portrayed. A university lecturer, an expert in their field, makes a mistake in their class, or in their lab—you won't find that on your news feed.

An athlete's mental health is as important as their physical health. There have been significant shifts in the public perception of mental health concerns and accessing treatment, but there is still a long way to go. Athletes need safe spaces where they feel empowered and supported so they can seek appropriate resources and ask for the help they need. Too often, athletes are perceived as showing weakness when discussing their mental health needs and concerns. They are often discounted or sometimes outright ignored. Depression and anxiety are as real as any physical injury and require evaluation and management by a qualified health professional.

The athletes' parents and coaches can start facilitating this process of validating mental health concerns by being open and listening to the athlete's issues and resisting the temptation to attempt to "fix" them or diminish their importance. Being an active, empathetic listener and providing pathways and access to appropriate mental health professionals can be a great next step. When or if an athlete discloses mental health concerns, be aware that this has taken great courage on their part and may be the first and only time they come forward asking for help. Don't let the opportunity pass you by.

SOCIAL CONSIDERATIONS

The social dynamics of sports also play an important role in the process of competitive excellence. All relationships have a social element, a human connection that can influence performance. In individual sports, this can be expressed through the coach-athlete relationship, but it's also expressed through social connections between the athlete and their opponents. We have discussed the importance of the opponent in competition, bringing out the best in you, driving performances that you could not create on your own, and that's real. But there are also opportunities for social connection between the moments of competition that can lead to friendship or, at the very least, camaraderie.

In team sports, the social connections are similar, but the inherent social dynamic is not limited to teams and teammates. Your opponents can play a role in helping everyone on a team become a better athlete and the team itself to become high functioning. Just as practice with teammates can up everyone's game, competing with your opponent can have that same effect. And improved performance isn't limited to scoring or athletic prowess; it also includes a full range of other important behaviors, such as sportsman-like conduct and emotional control. Remember, competing is to "strive or seek with" your opponent. There's a collaborative element in competition, and this is how it's expressed.

Rivalries between teams or individual players can be spectacular, fueling both athletes and fans as the intensity and level of play heats up. Rivalries can give athletes extra juice, but as valuable as that can be in the heat of competition, you don't want to allow your opponent to define you or your team. You want to define you. If a rival brings out the best in you, the challenge becomes figuring out how to elicit a similar level of energy, effort, and execution by yourself. Can you motivate intrinsically instead of relying on an external source? Remember, consistency is a critical part of sustained competitive success and if we play "up" for some opponents and play "down" to others, then we're letting them have far too much control over who we are in the moment of competition.

It's inevitable that you'll have conflict on teams. How you deal with it has a lot to do with the age of your athletes. Generally, conflicts are seen as me-versus-you exchanges that have the potential to disrupt the team and take energy away from the task at hand. A healthier perspective could be to view it as an "us" versus "the problem" exchange. As in, we're all in this together, so what affects one of us affects all of us, and therefore we should all work to resolve or solve the issue.

Disagreements happen, and in general I suggest that if you have a problem with someone, you address it directly with that person. Before your address them, though, start by first taking a look at yourself and trying to determine what role you played in the interaction. Think before you speak, and if you're too emotional to think rationally, take the time you need to formulate what you'd like to say before you say it. If you choose to initiate the discussion, start from a position of respect and honesty, do not personalize it.

If you're the person being talked to, let the person speaking finish what they have to say, and listen to understand as opposed to being defensive and listening to reply. Having heard what they've said, give your honest response and either resolve the issue and move on, or agree to disagree and move on. But, either way, move on. Grudges fester, and that discord will compromise trust and present itself at the most inopportune times.

Listen to what's being said, apologize sincerely for any distress your actions caused, take responsibility for your part in the interaction, and try to be done with it. If you still feel wronged or don't feel the issue has been resolved, you should try again for the betterment of everyone. Both parties should try to talk more to facilitate increased empathy or understanding to resolve the problem, or they could possibly enlist a trusted, neutral third party to help diffuse the situation. Keep working on issues until they are resolved. Make sure you can forgive, learn, and get back to the task at hand.

The other social consideration in all of this is social empathy. People are different. We all have a tendency to believe that our world perspective is right, but we only know our life's experiences. With over 7 billion people on the planet, how is our point of view more valid or correct than anyone else's? In a world that now promotes and supports diversity and inclusion, our ability to develop empathy for others is critical.

Empathy is only possible when you consider someone else's story as they experience it, not as you observe it. To that end, you have to meet people where they are, not where you think they should be, and while our perception might be our reality, we should understand that it might be different than others. And that's something we should be curious about, as opposed to being judgmental and dismissive.

Personal empathy is important, but cultural empathy is important too. There are behaviors that might seem rude or strange to you that are normal and accepted behaviors in other cultures (different nationalities, races, families, regions, religions, and so on). Because social norms are created by people, those who are part of a more prevalent culture tend to view their perceptions of others as correct and appropriate, which can also reduce empathy and understanding. Instead of viewing other people or cultures through the lens of judgment or assumption, we should consider being curious and respectful. Why do I think this? Is it true? Are my beliefs hurtful or oppressive? Do these beliefs create bias, and is this bias a barrier to empathy and understanding?

In addition to curiosity, we should also consider positivity. We tend to dehumanize the people we idolize, dislike, or don't know. This has become so much easier through anonymous and unfiltered digital communication. We demean and belittle and say things that we would never say directly to them. Seeing a person's face and their response to your words forces you to recognize their humanity and increases empathy. If you have something bad you want to say about someone, say it to their face. Saying it behind their back, or saying it behind a curtain of zeros and ones, is bad for you and for the person you're talking about. Take responsibility for your opinions and behaviors.

We should also try to think the best of people, give them the benefit of the doubt, whenever we can. When I assume that someone's intentions are good, or if I assume that poor intentions are driven by a bad experience, it increases the empathy I have for that person. For example, if someone cuts me off in traffic, I assume that it was an accident or maybe they need to get somewhere for an emergency. If someone says something that is clearly intentionally hurtful, I think, *They must be having a really bad day to say something like that. Maybe I should check in with them.* Leading with best assumptions can also increase empathy.

People are different, and those differences are a strength, especially when empathy is developed. There are numerous research articles that attest to quantifiable advantages in decision-making and problem-solving capabilities when diverse perspectives are added to teams and organizations.

Conclusion

Operating at the Center

What I've found, over the years, is that trying to become the best you can be, with the hope of achieving something significant, is a multifaceted process, and consequently, it requires a multifaceted approach. If you're an athlete, you have to work, learn, and compete. If you're a coach, you have to teach, coach, and mentor. But competitive excellence is not just about setting a lofty goal, acquiring and applying the required physical skills, planning and preparing to compete, emotional control and mental focus, creating high-functioning teams, or healthy social dynamics between athletes and coaches. It's about all of these things and, as you've read, a great many more. It's about acquiring all of the physical, mental, and social skills of competitive excellence and applying them to the moment of competition. Optimal performance and significant achievement result from developing strengths in each of these domains and harnessing the powerful synergies created by operating at the intersection of the all three—at the center:

THE CHAMPIONSHIP MODEL FOR CENTERED GOAL-SETTING

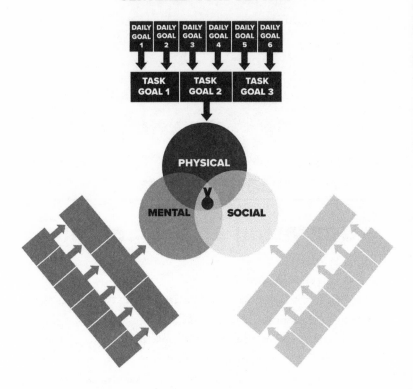

As I said in the introduction, our 2008 USA men's volleyball team worked hard over four years and learned how to operate at the center. It all came together as we'd hoped and planned, but the outcome was never guaranteed. Even though we were playing our best when our best was needed, we were never a "lock" to win gold.

To me, becoming Olympic champions was something you dreamed about; it wasn't something you actually did. With all of the belief I had in our process and the faith I had in our staff and athletes, I didn't actually dare to think about the outcome until we won a rally in the fourth set in the final against Brazil. We led 24–22 at that point, up two sets to one. (Volleyball is scored by best three sets out of five, each set to 25 points, win by two, with the fifth set played to 15 points). At that moment, I remember quite distinctly having this sudden and surreal thought, *We could actually win!* I briefly turned away from the court to take a breath and try to get my heart rate down from the 180 bpm it had suddenly risen to. I pulled myself together and got back to the task at hand, saying and doing everything I could to help the team win that next point.

We served, and Brazil scored, making it 24–23. We received serve for the match and played the last point to perfection. We competed with composure and made the right choices and the right plays to win, just as we'd practiced and planned.

A few hours after the medal ceremony, I was on a plane heading home. We'd done what we'd set out to do, and my time and energy were needed elsewhere. The team left the next day to report to their professional clubs. Our four years to be good for two weeks to be great for the last two hours were over, and everyone got on with the next chapter of lives.

Achieving these significant outcomes in sports is challenging. If you choose to compete, then understand your opponent will say and do everything they can to beat you. They will find and exploit any weaknesses that you have, and they will also have plans in place to neutralize your strengths. In addition, the contest will be played out in the public arena for any and all to see. It all gets "real" in a hurry.

The narrative on improvement and the dream of achieving significant outcomes is that you work hard through each level of the process, and then, finally, you arrive. You achieve the goal, you "make it" and then, somehow, your life will be transformed. There'll be rainbows and ponies everywhere, and you will lay your head down each night on a pillow made of kitten's dreams. It will be magical!

Not to spoil it for everyone, but it doesn't quite work that way. The truth is that you never really arrive, you just keep moving forward. You might achieve some significant outcomes, and there's immense satisfaction to be had in that, perhaps even pride, but what's done is done, and we have to take care of the here and now.

The message we hear growing up is that gold medals are the most sacred of all sporting accomplishments, that they change your stars. In some ways, they do, but just not in the way the world tells us. Don't get me wrong, it is deeply and profoundly satisfying to become an Olympic champion, but when you look at the whole U.S. Olympic team, there will usually be about 90 gold medalists at the Summer Games, and more coming in two years with the Winter Games. There's just not enough room on the Wheaties box for everyone. Those who win silver or bronze are quickly dismissed. The expectations are, without question, way too high. So high, in fact, they can diminish the accomplishment itself. Many athletes feel disillusioned because they are "promised" that the outcome leads to more outcomes. The medal leads to endorsements and ticker tape and TV appearances, which it does, but just not for everyone. Gold medals might change the lives of a few, but for many Olympic champions, life is a little bit different the day after they win, but not a lot.

The idea of "arriving" is dangerous in a different way as well. Apart from the disappointment of finding yourself still encumbered by the human condition, we can be tricked in our pursuit of significant outcomes into treating time as a commodity. For example, we might give away years of our childhood to youth sports, years that we will never get back, for the promise of a better tomorrow. But will our tomorrow really be better?

We can't say, but we are not guaranteed that tomorrow. The universe certainly doesn't owe it to us, nor are we entitled to it. The promise of a better tomorrow tricks us into giving away our todays, and today is the only sure thing we have, so as John Wooden said, "We should make it our masterpiece."

Todays can not only be sullied by tomorrows, they can be influenced by our yesterdays as well. As we experience life, mistakes and moments of adversity will undoubtedly occur. Our inclination will be to dwell on these moments, ruminate, lick our wounds, or grieve, and we should. The question, though, is how long? How long are we going to hold onto that pain or discomfort? How many todays will be a little bit less because of our yesterday? We have a responsibility to ourselves to live each day as best we can, with best effort and best intention, honoring the significant relationships in our lives, and drinking deeply from the cup of humanity. There are no guarantees in life, every day actually is a gift, an opportunity, so make the most of it.

It is my hope that this book does some good. That it stimulates some thought, maybe even some discussion, and that it helps people. In a sporting world that's often complicated, perhaps it can provide some clarity and direction relative to what the process of competitive excellence and significant achievement looks like. If you're an athlete, you now understand what it is to work, learn, and compete. If you're a coach, you are now better equipped to teach, coach, and mentor. If you're the parent of an athlete, you have a better idea of what to look for when choosing the person or program that will oversee your athlete's development.

No matter who you are, though, or why you're reading this, the time for reading is done. It's time to dream a little, to hope for something that captures your head and your heart, and then get to work. Commit to the process of competitive excellence, acquire and apply these championship behaviors, and do your best to achieve your significant outcome. You'll be good enough or you won't, but whatever the result, you'll be better for it. You'll be better at sports, you'll be better at life, and you'll help those around you to be better as well. When you choose to operate at the center, you learn to become the champion of yourself, and there's no greater achievement than that.

Notes

1. According to 2022 data from BachelorsPortal.com.
2. https://scholarshipstats.com/average-per-athlete.
3. K. Anders Ericsson, "Enhancing the Development of Professional Performance: Implications from the Study of Deliberate Practice," *Development of Professional Expertise Toward Measurement of Expert Performance and Design of Optimal Learning Environments* (Cambridge University Press, 2009). p. 406 (entire article is Chapter 18, p. 405–431); DOI: https://doi.org/10.1017/CBO9780511609817.022
4. Benjamin S. Bloom (Editor), *Developing Talent in Young People* (New York: Ballantine Books), 1985, p. 473.
5. Definition of the Society of Human Resource Management; https://www.shrm.org/resourcesandtools/tools-and-samples/toolkits/pages/developingandsustaininghigh-performanceworkteams.aspx.
6. Edwin A. Locke and Judith F. Bryan, "Goal-setting as a determinant of the effect of knowledge of score on performance," *The American Journal of Psychology*, 1968; 81(3), 398–406. https://doi.org/10.2307/1420637.
7. B. Ann Boyce, "Effects of Goal Specificity and Goal Difficulty upon Skill Acquisition of a Selected Shooting Task," *Perceptual and Motor Skills*, First Published June 1, 1990; Research Article; and Damon Burton, "Winning Isn't Everything: Examining the Impact

of Performance Goals on Collegiate Swimmers' Cognitions and Performance," *The Sport Psychologist*; DOI: https://doi.org/10.1123/tsp.3.2.105.

8. Paul Caldarella, Ross A.A. Larsen, Leslie Williams, Kade R. Downs, Howard P. Wills, and Joseph H. Wehby, "Effects of teachers' praise-to-reprimand ratios on elementary students' on-task behavior," *Educational Psychology*, Volume 20, 2020 (Issue 10), January 29, 2020; p. 1306–1322.

9. Alden Gonzalez, "How Cooper Kupp went from no college offers to several college records," ESPN.com, July 27, 2017; https://www.espn.com/blog/los-angeles-rams/post/_/id/34382/how-cooper-kupp-went-from-no-college-offers-to-several-college-records.

10. Piers Steel, "Hard Work Beats Talent (But Only If Talent Doesn't Work Hard)," *Psychology Today*, October 8, 2011; https://www.psychologytoday.com/us/blog/the-procrastination-equation/201110/hard-work-beats-talent-only-if-talent-doesn-t-work-hard.

11. Paul Morris Fitts and Michael I. Posner, *Human Performance* (Basic Concepts in Psychology Series) (Brooks/Cole, 1967).

12. Ann M. Gentile, "A Working Model of Skill Acquisition with Application to Teaching," *Quest*, Vol. 17(1):3–23. DOI: 10.1080/00336297.1972.10519717.

13. John Nixon, and Lawrence Locke, "Research on teaching physical education," *Second Handbook of Research on Teaching*, (Ed. R. Travers) (Rand McNally and Company, 1973).

14. Richard A. Schmidt, "A schema theory of discrete motor skill learning," *Psychological Review* (1975); 82(4), 225–260. https://doi.org/10.1037/h0076770.

15. K.A. Ericcson, W.G. Chase, and S. Faloon, "Acquisition of a memory skill," *Science*, June 6, 1980; 208(4448):1181–2. doi: 10.1126/science.7375930; PMID: 7375930 DOI: 10.1126/science.7375930.

16. Ericsson, K. Anders Krampe, Ralf T. Tesch-Römer, Clemens, "The role of deliberate practice in the acquisition of expert

performance," *Psychological Review*, 100(3), 363–406. https://doi.
org/10.1037/0033-295X.100.3.363.

17. Gabriele Wulf, Nathan McConnel, Matthias Gärtner, and Andreas
Schwarz, "Enhancing the Learning of Sport Skills Through
External-Focus Feedback," *Journal of Motor Behavior*, 2002,
Vol. 34, No. 2, 171–182.

18. Stephen Wolfram, *A New Kind of Science* (Wolfram Media; 1st
edition, 2002).

19. René Marois and Jason Ivanoff, "Capacity limits of information
processing in the brain," *TRENDS in Cognitive Science*, Vol. 9,
No. 6 June 2005.

20. Miller, *Ibid.*

21. A. W. Salmoni, R.A. Schmidt, and C.B. Walter, "Knowledge of
results and motor learning: a review and critical reappraisal,
Psychological Bulletin, May 1984; 95(3):355–86.

22. Mikaela Shiffrin in an interview with NBC News Chicago
February 14, 2022, "Mikaela Shiffrin: Her Olympic Focus,
Athlete Pressure and a Heartbreaking Loss;"
https://www.nbcchicago.com/news/sports/beijing-
winter-olympics/mikaela-shiffrin-her-olympic-focus-
athlete-expectations-and-a-heartbreaking-loss/2759343/#:~:
text=%E2%80%9CI'm%20not%20focusing%20on,best%20
shot%20at%20a%20medal.

23. "Why is the news always so depressing? The Negativity Bias
explained," The Decision Lab; https://thedecisionlab.com/biases/
negativity-bias/#section-10.

24. Viktor Frankl, *Man's Search for Meaning* (Reprint) (Beacon, 2006).
Frankl, who spent three years in concentrations camps during
World War II, was a professor of neurology and psychiatry until
his death in 1997.

25. F.M. Henry, "Specificity vs. generality in learning motor skills,"
Proceedings of the College Physical Education Association,
Washington, DC., 1958.

26. Lisa M. Guth and Stephen M. Roth, "Genetic influence on athletic performance," Current Opinion in Pediatrics 2013 Dec; 25(6): 653–658; doi: 10.1097/MOP.0b013e3283659087; https://www. ncbi.nlm.nih.gov/pmc/articles/PMC3993978.

27. Edwin A. Fleischman, *The Structure and Measurement of Physical Fitness* (Prentice Hall, 1965).

28. George Leonard, *Mastery: The Keys to Success and Long-term Fulfillment* (Dutton, 1991).

29. Maryann Karinch, *Lessons from the Edge* (Simon & Schuster, 2000).

30. David Epstein, *Range: Why Generalists Triumph in a Specialized World* (Riverhead Books, 2019).

31. Steve Peters, *The Chimp Paradox: The Mind Management Program to Help You Achieve Success, Confidence, and Happiness* (TarcherPerigee, 2013).

32. Mihaly Csikszentmihalyi, *Flow: The Psychology of Optimal Experience* (Harper Perennial Modern Classics, 2008).

33. Bloom, *Ibid.*

34. Alfie Kohn, *No Contest: The Case Against Competition* (Houghton Mifflin, 1992).

35. David Light Shields and Brenda Light Bredemeier, *True Competition: A Guide to Pursuing Excellence in Sport and Society* (Human Kinetics, 2009).

36. Roy F. Baumeister, "Choking under pressure: Self-consciousness and paradoxical effects of incentives on skillful performance," *Journal of Personality and Social Psychology* (1984); 46(3), 610–620.

37. Howard Fendrich, "Shiffrin talks about watching Biles deal with Olympic stress," Associated Press, February 2, 2022; https://apnews.com/article/winter-olympics-mikaela-shiffrin-mental-health-simone-biles-d1e8b3b25a6744739eb016d b2f715188.